Advance Praise

"What a fabulous book! The interventions and implementation strategies presented in this text have the potential to profoundly impact the educational experiences of students with disabilities and their peers. I hope that teachers and teacher-licensure students all across the country have the opportunity to read this book and put it into practice."

—Elizabeth E. Biggs, PhD, Vanderbilt University

"This book tackles key barriers to inclusion, including strategies to support paraeducators, along with proven methods to engage peers in building inclusive communities with their classmates with disabilities. Four peer-based interventions are thoughtfully outlined for practitioners, along with case examples, practical how-to guides, and resources that can be used immediately in the classroom. Brock does a terrific job in making research evidence usable for classroom staff—a critical step in reducing the research-to-practice gaps that interfere with building inclusive settings. This book fosters competence, confidence, and connectedness for *all* staff and students."

—Kara Hume, associate professor, School of Education,
University of North Carolina–Chapel Hill

"One of the most important strategies for ensuring students with complex needs become members of inclusive and effective educational communities is to facilitate systems of peer supports. In this book, Dr. Brock draws upon both his teaching and extensive research experience to provide a roadmap for educators hoping to increase their students' access and success in inclusive classrooms through peer supports. This book is comprehensive, yet accessible and practical; it will certainly be a valuable resource for preservice and seasoned educators alike. Dr. Brock has also provided essential guidance on supporting paraeducators in inclusive classrooms, an important topic often insufficiently addressed in teacher education programs. I hope this book finds its way onto the shelf of every general and special educator!"

—Robert Pennington, PhD, BCBA-D, Lake & Edward J. Snyder, Jr.
Distinguished Professor in special education,
University of North Carolina–Charlotte

"We've known for years that peer interventions can benefit all students in inclusive settings; however, several challenges continue to impede the implementation of this evidence-based strategy. Using plain language, this book clearly identifies the most prevalent challenges and provides practical recommendations for preemptively troubleshooting issues in order to effectively embed peer interventions throughout the school setting. Organized into two parts and seven chapters, it systematically describes how to partner with paraeducators and peers, with a focus on modeling, coaching, and feedback. The text details how to select and implement appropriate interventions through vignettes, activities, checklists, and blank consumable forms with detailed step-by-step directives for immediate use. For anyone looking to build sustainable and effective inclusionary practices, this book is an absolute must-have!"

—**Luann Ley Davis**, PhD, associate professor of special education,
University of Memphis

"Brock's necessary book provides educators with easy-to-follow strategies to engage some of the most valuable and under-supported partners for children and youth with disabilities: paraprofessionals and peers. Brock respects educators' needs and distills these strategies to their most essential features. Reflective questions at critical points of each of the four peer-focused, evidence-based interventions prepare educators to make decisions ensuring success for students with and without disabilities."

—**Suzanne Kucharczyk**, associate professor of special education,
University of Arkansas

"*It Isn't Inclusion Without Peers* provides a new and important viewpoint on supporting inclusive practices for children with disabilities: involving peers without disabilities. Packed with practical guidance for educators with any level of experience, the easy-to-read text highlights how to best partner with peers and use paraeducators to facilitate peer involvement. Educators will also be guided in selecting and implementing peer-focused interventions. A must-read text for teachers looking to implement sustainable inclusion practices."

—**Sarah N. Douglas**, PhD, associate professor and RADD lab director,
Michigan State University

IT ISN'T INCLUSION
WITHOUT PEERS

**The Norton Series on Inclusive Education
for Students with Disabilities**
Michael L. Wehmeyer and Jennifer A. Kurth, series editors

The Series on Inclusive Education for Students with Disabilities is a publishing home for books that offer strengths-based approaches to understanding disability and that propose educational supports to enable all students, with and without disabilities, to succeed. Books in the series provide practical, research-referenced information for educators who teach students with disabilities in typical education contexts with their nondisabled peers.

It Isn't Inclusion Without Peers
Matthew E. Brock

Build Equity, Join Justice
Amy B. McCart, Wade Kelly, and Wayne Sailor

Planning for the Success of Students with IEPs
James R. Thompson

Inclusive Education in a Strengths-Based Era
Michael L. Wehmeyer and Jennifer A. Kurth

Norton Books in Education

IT ISN'T INCLUSION
WITHOUT PEERS

SUPPORTING STUDENTS WITH AND WITHOUT
DISABILITIES TO LEARN TOGETHER

MATTHEW E. BROCK

Norton Professional Books

An Imprint of W. W. Norton & Company
Celebrating a Century of Independent Publishing

For information about permission to reproduce selections from this book, write to Permissions, W. W. Norton & Company, Inc., 500 Fifth Avenue, New York, NY 10110

For information about special discounts for bulk purchases, please contact W. W. Norton Special Sales at specialsales@wwnorton.com or 800-233-4830

Manufacturing by Versa Press
Production manager: Gwen Cullen

ISBN: 978-1-324-03075-1 (pbk)

W. W. Norton & Company, Inc., 500 Fifth Avenue, New York, NY 10110
www.wwnorton.com

W. W. Norton & Company Ltd., 15 Carlisle Street, London W1D 3BS

1 2 3 4 5 6 7 8 9 0

To my sister, Lori Brock,
who is the reason I entered this field

Contents

Acknowledgments

All of my research on peer-mediated intervention and paraeducator training has been a team effort. I want to thank the many people who have contributed to this research, including Hannah Rogers, Sara Martin, Tzu-Jung Lin, Ann O'Connell, Max Bloodworth, Taylor Gleason, Pam Crum, Kara Shawbitz, Sara Hudler, Jenna Hurlburt, Kaitlyn Viera, Kate Anderson, Scott Dueker, Eric Anderson, Xiaoning Sun, Mary Barczak, Rachel Seaman-Tullis, John Schaefer, Chelsea Amadi, Kelsey Trausch, Morgan Herbert, Courtney Downing, Lauryn Wermer, Andrea Ranney, Lauren Beaman-Diglia, Heartley Huber, and Elizabeth Biggs.

I want to thank all of the administrators who have allowed us to work in their schools, the teachers who have welcomed us into their classrooms, the families who have allowed us to work with their children, and the students who have participated in our research. Specifically, I want to thank Columbus City Schools, Dublin City Schools, Gahanna-Jefferson Schools, Olentangy Local Schools, Pickerington Local Schools, and Reynoldsburg City Schools.

I also want to thank all of the senior researchers who have mentored me, including Erik Carter, Sam Odom, Deborah Hatton, and Laura Justice.

Finally, I want to thank the team at Norton who worked with me to publish this book. In particular, I want to thank Carol Collins, whose suggestions and feedback made this a clearer and better organized text.

IT ISN'T INCLUSION
WITHOUT PEERS

PART I

PARTNERING WITH PEERS AND PARAEDUCATORS

There is a popular narrative—both among scholars and in the mainstream media—that inclusion has become the most common form of education for students with disabilities (Gilmour, 2018). This narrative is half true. Students with the mildest disabilities have indeed experienced steady progress toward being educated primarily in regular education classrooms alongside peers without disabilities. Over the past 25 years, the proportion of students with specific learning disabilities who are included in regular education classrooms has more than tripled (Williamson et al., 2020). This progress has been celebrated by advocates for students with specific learning disabilities and their families, and rightfully so.

However, when it comes to students with significant disabilities, this narrative gets turned on its head. For students with developmental disabilities such as intellectual disability, autism, or multiple disabilities, the data paint a very different picture. At a national level, the rate of inclusion for students with intellectual disability has flatlined over the last

20 years (Brock, 2018). In every year for the past 40 years, the majority of students with intellectual disability have spent most or all of their day in separate classrooms or schools. Similar trends have been observed for students with other low incidence disabilities as well as students with multiple disabilities (Kurth et al., 2014). Digging more deeply into the data raises even more concerns, as some states and school districts are trending toward *less* inclusion for students with significant disabilities. For example, in states like Montana, Massachusetts, and Vermont, students with significant disabilities are less likely to be included than they were 20 years ago (Anderson & Brock, 2020). Indeed, the data clearly show that segregated classrooms and schools have always been and continue to be the dominant form of education for students with significant disabilities in the United States.

From my own experiences as a teacher and educational researcher, I offer a simple explanation for why most students with significant disabilities are not included: inclusion can be hard. In many schools, teachers feel like they are swimming against the current as they work to include their students. Once a school system has invested in separate classrooms and schools, these settings often become the unspoken default placement for students with significant disabilities and the path of least resistance (Brock & Schaefer, 2015). Even when teachers, families, and administrators decide together that a student will be included, teachers face challenges in promoting meaningful inclusion.

My work focuses on two of these challenges. First, teachers need feasible and practical strategies to promote high-quality inclusion. Too often, teacher preparation programs emphasize a theoretical argument for inclusion but do too little to prepare future teachers in practical approaches. This can leave teachers unsure how to support students in inclusive classrooms and other settings. Furthermore, when teachers try to place students in regular education classrooms without having the right supports in place, it is discouraging when students flounder—making it less likely that teachers will advocate for inclusive opportunities in the future. Second, the success of inclusion often hinges on partnerships with paraeducators, whom many teachers feel underprepared to coach and supervise. Teachers report a lack of training in their preservice teacher education program on how to work with paraeducators and a lack of confidence in how to go about providing effective coaching and supervision (Biggs et al., 2016).

In my own experience as a teacher, I have struggled with both of these barriers. I entered the field passionate about inclusion but unsure of how to make it happen. I learned quickly that simply placing a student in a regular education classroom was inadequate and that I needed to take steps to ensure that students with disabilities had opportunities to meaningfully interact with peers and to fully participate in classroom activities. Like many teachers who encounter a challenge for which they do not already have a solution, I spent a lot of time trying out new ideas, continuing with the ones that worked well, and discarding the ones that did not. Over time, I changed my perspective about how I approached supporting inclusion. At first, I had focused almost entirely on ensuring that adults provided students with the best individualized supports. I thought that inclusion was at its best when teachers made good decisions about accommodations and modifications and when teachers and paraeducators delivered highly individualized instruction. Later, I realized that while these things were important, I was missing a critical piece of the puzzle: peers. Inclusion is about building a community where students build relationships with their peers and learn together. Instead of focusing solely on adult-to-student interactions, I broadened my focus to how adults can facilitate interactions and learning among students with significant disabilities and their peers.

In addition, I realized in my first years of teaching that I was woefully underprepared to manage a team of paraeducators. Fresh out of an undergraduate program, I struggled with how to lead a team of adults. I was intimidated by the fact that some paraeducators on my team were over twice my age and had already had long careers in education. My teacher preparation program did a wonderful job preparing me to use instructional strategies with children, but little to guide me in coaching and supervising other adults.

These experiences from teaching shape my current work as a researcher. My research agenda is aligned with the same two barriers I faced as a teacher—practical strategies for promoting meaningful inclusion and effective coaching and supervision of paraeducators. I work with a research team to learn more about these issues through scientific research. Together, we partner with teachers and paraeducators in schools to develop, test, and improve practical solutions. We work with teachers who coach and supervise paraeducators who support students with significant disabilities in inclusive classrooms, lunchrooms, and on the playground. We train and support these teachers and paraeducators to partner with peers to promote meaningful interactions and learning while decreasing overreliance on adults. Through rigorous research methods, we seek to identify the best strategies for promoting meaningful inclusion and the best approaches for coaching paraeducators to use these strategies effectively. In addition, my research team surveys and interviews teachers to gain their perspective. We ask them what they think of our interventions, whether they plan to continue using them, and what recommendations they have for us. Our goal is to develop approaches that improve outcomes for students with significant disabilities and that are feasible and sustainable for teachers to implement.

Although I am still learning, I know much more today about supporting inclusion through peer-mediated intervention and coaching paraeducators than I did as a teacher. This book is a culmination of what I have learned to date from my own work as well as the work of my colleagues who conduct similar research. Because I know from my own experience that teachers are looking for answers and have limited time, I have designed this text be succinct and efficient. It includes tools that I wish I had had as a teacher—practical approaches for promoting meaningful inclusion while partnering with paraeducators. I hope this text makes your journey as a teacher a little easier.

1

Why Involve Students Without Disabilities?

For nearly 50 years, federal law has mandated that students with significant disabilities be educated alongside their peers without disabilities to the maximum extent possible (Individuals With Disabilities Education Improvement Act [IDEIA], 2004). This mandate is in place for good reason. Inclusion provides access to an invaluable resource that cannot be found in self-contained classrooms or specialized schools. This invaluable resource is peers. When surrounded by peers without disabilities, students have a wealth of natural opportunities to observe, learn, and practice communication and social skills (Dell'Anna et al., 2020). Similarly, peers naturally provide students with models of everyday skills and classroom routines (Kurth et al., 2015). Furthermore, students with significant disabilities make more progress on the academic curriculum when they learn alongside peers without disabilities (Coyne et al., 2012). In sum, peers are the key ingredient that transforms schools into inclusive learning environments. In other words, it isn't inclusion without peers.

Surprisingly, peers are not always a prominent focus of efforts to include students with significant disabilities. When peers are not part of the conversation, students can be present without being meaningfully included. In too many classrooms, students with significant disabilities sit on the periphery, primarily interacting with special education support staff instead of with peers or the general education teacher (Trausch et al., 2021). On too many playgrounds, students with disabilities spend recess playing only by themselves, missing out on rich opportunities for developing play and social skills (Brock, Shawbitz et al., 2021). In too many school cafeterias, these students sit at tables by themselves or exclusively with support staff and other students with disabilities, missing out on opportunities to talk and build social connections with peers (Herbert et al., 2020). Clearly, being in the same physical space does not automatically translate into meaningful engagement with peers. Students with significant disabilities will experience the full benefits of inclusion only when strategies are in place to promote positive interactions and cooperation with peers.

The need to support interactions between students with significant disabilities and their peers should not come as a surprise. When it comes to navigating the social landscape, students with significant disabilities start out at a deficit and are given limited opportunities to catch up. Compared to students from other disability groups, students with intellectual disability, autism, or multiple disabilities are at the highest risk for deficits in social and communication skills (Matson et al., 2009). In addition, these students have very limited opportunities to socialize. While peers have the entire school day to interact and build relationships, most students with significant disabilities spend less than 40% of the school day in the same space as peers (Brock et al., 2018). These challenges are exacerbated when school staff support students in ways that make peer interactions even less likely. When assigned to support a student, staff frequently presume that they should sit next to the student, and often this is most convenient on the periphery of a classroom or lunchroom. When students are seated far away from peers and constantly shadowed by an adult, spontaneous peer interactions are even less likely to occur (Giangreco, 2010). These challenges underscore the critical need to intentionally promote positive interaction and cooperation between students with significant disabilities and their peers.

Peer-mediated interventions provide a practical solution to this problem. Peer-mediated interventions are a group of practices in which adults coach peers to interact with and provide support to students with significant disabilities in inclusive classrooms, lunchrooms, and on the playground. These interventions are designed to mutually benefit both students with disabilities and the peers who provide support. Benefits for the students with disabilities include increased peer interaction; increased engagement in the general education curriculum; decreased overreliance on adults; and increased progress on individualized goals targeting communication, social, and academic skills (Brock & Huber,

2017; Trausch et al., 2021). Benefits for the peers include increased engagement in class activities; the learning of new skills, such as sign language; increased comfort interacting with people with disabilities; and improved confidence and feelings of self-worth (Travers & Carter, 2022). And when peer-mediated interventions contribute to a school environment that is more inclusive and accepting, everyone benefits. Peer-mediated interventions should not be considered an optional or supplemental approach. They are the only proven means to promote meaningful and mutually beneficial interactions between students with significant disabilities and their peers.

More is known today than ever before about how to effectively support positive interactions between students with significant disabilities and their peers. While researchers have studied peer-mediated interventions for decades, the amount of research on this topic has sharply proliferated in recent years. Currently, there is sufficient high-quality research for scholars to confidently make claims about which peer-focused interventions are evidence-based or strongly linked with improved student outcomes (Brock & Huber, 2017). In addition, researchers have worked to specialize different peer-mediate interventions for different goals and situations. For example, interventions can be designed to target academic outcomes, social outcomes, or both. Also, interventions have been designed for different contexts, such as classrooms, the lunchroom, or recess. Given this menu of effective approaches, teachers can select the peer-mediated intervention that is the best match for a specific student and situation.

The goal of this book is to give teachers a practical guide to peer-mediated interventions that is grounded in what scholars have learned from decades of research. Given that most teachers will need to team up with paraeducators to successfully use these practices, Chapter 2 focuses on strategies for effectively training and coaching paraeducators to implement peer-mediated interventions. Principles from this chapter are integrated into later chapters on how to implement specific interventions. The introduction to Part II provides a guide for selecting the peer-mediated intervention that is the best match for specific students and situations. Chapters 3 through 6 provide detailed step-by-step guides and resources for planning and using four different peer-mediated interventions. Each chapter includes an overview of the intervention, a description of students whom it would benefit most, step-by-step directions, strategies for troubleshooting when things do not go as planned, research-based approaches for partnering with paraeducators, and vignettes, based on real students, that illustrate what the intervention looks like in action. Finally, the last chapter provides guidance on how to combine peer-mediated interventions to support inclusion throughout the school day. With these tools, teachers can build inclusive schools that enable students with and without disabilities to learn, play, and grow together.

2

Teaming With Paraeducators

Today's special education teachers find themselves in a unique predicament. On one hand, teachers have more adult help than ever before. Schools continue to hire the same numbers of special education teachers while increasing the number of paraeducators who are hired to support them (U.S. Department of Education, 2022). On the other hand, teachers have been thrust into the role of training, supervising, and coaching paraeducators—a challenging responsibility that many teachers feel underprepared to perform (Frantz et al., 2022). This responsibility can feel even more daunting when teachers deploy paraeducators to multiple classrooms to support the inclusion of students with disabilities. It is impossible for teachers to be in more than one place at the same time, and keeping tabs on what is happening with students in different classrooms can feel overwhelming.

Fortunately, there are practical solutions for meeting these challenges that are proven through research. This chapter includes an overview of what researchers have learned after years of studying paraeducator training and supervision. There is sufficient evidence that researchers have come to a consensus about which approaches are—and are not—effective (Brock & Anderson, 2021). This chapter reviews approaches that do not work, approaches that do work, and strategies for how teachers can balance effective paraeducator training and supervision with their other responsibilities. See Table 2.1 for an overview of what does and does not work in paraeducator training.

TABLE 2.1 What Does and Does Not Work in Paraeducator Training

WHAT DOES NOT WORK	WHAT DOES WORK
• Ambiguous expectations	• Clearly defined roles
• One-and-done workshops	• Initial training followed by sustained coaching with performance feedback
• Loosely organized training	• Training that is aligned with an implementation checklist
• Only talking about a practice	• Modeling what a practice looks like in action
• Focusing solely on how to implement a practice without talking about why	• Framing training around how the practice will benefit the student

What Does Not Work

First, the bad news: The training that many paraeducators receive is woefully inadequate. Many paraeducators report being tasked to support students with significant disabilities in inclusive classrooms without receiving *any* training on how to do so (Lichte & Scheef, 2022). Roles and responsibilities are not clearly defined, so these paraeducators are left to themselves to imagine what inclusion should look like and how they should support it. In other words, an individual with no background or training is entrusted with taking on a pivotal role with little direction or oversight. Unsurprisingly, things often do not go well. Unclear on what they are expected to do, many paraeducators mistakenly presume they should do as many things as possible *for* the student—including things that the student could do for themselves. Paraeducators might also mistakenly presume that they should be tethered to the student and that the most convenient place to sit with the student is on the periphery of the classroom away from peers. This inevitably leads to overdependence on adults and little to no interaction with peers (Carter et al., 2008). Furthermore, in a well-meaning effort to keep students engaged, paraeducators sometimes bring independent work for the student that is not aligned with what the rest of the class is learning. In the absence of training or a clearly defined role, these paraeducators are inadvertently taking actions that are counterproductive to the primary goals of inclusion—that is, building independence, supporting social and communication development, and promoting access to the general education curriculum. The absence of adequate training is both unethical and inconsistent with the law, which requires paraeducators to provide support only after receiving appropriate training (IDEIA, 2004).

Even when paraeducators do receive training, it is rarely well designed. The most popular form of paraeducator training is what scholars have dubbed "one-and-done" professional development (Wiggs et al., 2021). For example, a paraeducator might go to a half-day training focused on a specific strategy or collection of strategies. They sit passively as someone lectures to them. Afterward, there is no follow-up support, and paraeducators are left to sort out for themselves how to apply what they learned to meet the unique support needs of a student. For any adult, it is very difficult to master a new skill without ever seeing the skill in action or getting feedback from someone with experience. Indeed, there is good reason why all teacher preparation programs require student teaching experiences wherein preservice teachers observe a veteran teacher and then take increasing responsibility for teaching with the benefit of close supervision and coaching. In sum, it is unreasonable to expect paraeducators to skillfully support the inclusion of students with significant disabilities after a one-and-done training.

At this point, some readers might be thinking of individual paraeducators who have made tremendous contributions to supporting inclusion despite only receiving one-and-done training or little training at all. Indeed, some teachers are lucky enough to partner with paraeducators who are naturally talented and have past experiences that guide their understanding of supporting inclusion. However, the success of these exceptional individuals in no way justifies a clack of well-designed professional development. All paraeducators deserve and benefit from high-quality training and supervision—especially those who are already finding a way to be successful in spite of its absence.

What Does Work

The good news is that evidence from research points to a collection of training and supervision practices that enable paraeducators to implement effective support practices for students with significant disabilities in inclusive classrooms. These practices include clearly defining what is expected, explaining how an approach will improve student outcomes, providing written instruc-

tions, explaining and modeling those instructions, and then observing and providing constructive feedback (Brock & Anderson, 2021). Described below in
detail, these practices form the basis for the guidance throughout this book on
training and coaching paraeducators.

Defining Roles

A prerequisite to effective training is a clear definition of the paraeducator's
role. This involves clarifying how responsibilities for teachers and paraeducators differ. In the context of peer-mediated interventions in inclusive classrooms,
a teacher's role should involve designing support, coaching the paraeducator to
implement supports as designed, monitoring the effectiveness of supports, and
directing the paraeducator to make adjustments as needed. A paraeducator's
role may include providing input as the teacher designs supports, implementing
supports as directed, collecting data as directed, and communicating regularly
with the teacher. With this in mind, teachers should design supports and data
collection procedures prior to training paraeducators, and then provide initial
training and coaching that aligns with these roles.

Initial Training

Initial training introduces paraeducators to the practice that they will be implementing and sets them up for initial success. There are three key components
associated with effective initial training, including highlighting benefits for the
student, walking through a checklist of implementation steps, and modeling the
steps for the paraeducator.

Highlight Benefits for the Student. The first component is focused on *why*
teachers are directing paraeducators to implement a given practice. This
includes explaining what the practice is designed to do and why the practice is a
good match for the student and the inclusive classroom. Starting with potential
benefits for the student provides a clear picture of the end goal before charting
a course to get there. Having the end goal in mind can be motivating for paraeducators, and they may find it helpful to frame their thinking around what the
practice is designed to do.

Walk Through a Checklist. The next critical component is walking through a checklist that describes each step of the practice. Sometimes this will involve numbered steps that must be completed in a specific order, and other times items will be implemented as needed, contingent on what the student is doing or on what is happening in the classroom. An implementation checklist is helpful in three ways. First, it helps teachers provide complete and consistent training. With a checklist in hand, teachers can make sure they do not miss any important information during the initial training. Later when providing feedback, teachers can be certain they are linking to the same information that they initially shared. Second, reading over a checklist helps prime paraeducators before using a practice. As with many other tasks, having a to-do list can help maintain focus on what is important. Third, paraeducators can use checklists to monitor their own performance by checking off steps as they complete them. Teachers walk through the checklist by reading each step, talking through what is involved, and checking with the paraeducator for understanding.

Model the Steps. Most things are easier to do after watching someone else do it first. Often, the most straightforward way to model implementation steps is for the teacher to use the practice with the student as the paraeducator observes. While modeling, the implementation checklist can be a helpful reference both for the teacher, to ensure they are modeling all steps correctly, and for the paraeducator, to help them match the written steps to what they look like in action.

Ongoing Coaching With Observation and Feedback

After the initial training, paraeducators are familiar with why a practice is being used, what steps are involved, and what the steps look like. However, this is just the starting point. The most powerful tool for paraeducator training is ongoing coaching that features performance feedback (Brock et al., 2017). This involves a teacher observing a paraeducator and providing feedback about what was done well and what could be improved. When identifying implementation steps that could be improved, it can be helpful for teachers to model those steps again for the paraeducator—drawing attention to the aspect of implementation being targeted for improvement. Linking feedback to the checklist helps keep coaching focused on the key components of the practice. Two critical features of coaching are that it begins immediately after initial training and that it is sustained over time. In research studies, weekly coaching sessions have been sufficient to enable paraeducators to improve their implementation of a new practice (Brock, Barczak, et al., 2021).

Balancing Paraeducator Training and Supervision With Other Responsibilities

Time is often the primary obstacle to training and coaching paraeducators to implement peer-mediated interventions (Wallace et al., 2001). For initial training, it can be difficult to identify a time when a teacher and paraeducator can meet during the school day while others are available to supervise students. Paraeducators are not always paid for working before children arrive at or after children leave the school, so these might not be feasible options. For coaching, teachers may not always be able to leave the special education classroom to observe paraeducators. After all, a paraeducator is usually tasked with supporting a student in an inclusive classroom because the teacher is busy working with other students.

When struggling to overcome the obstacle of time, there are number of practical solutions. First, teachers should talk with the school building administrator who oversees special education—often a principal or assistant principal. It can be helpful to come to this conversation with a clear request and rationale. For example, "If you can help me to get coverage in my classroom for 45 minutes, I can train my team in strategies that are proven to improve outcomes for students with significant disabilities in inclusive classrooms. I am really excited about what this could mean for our students, and my team is not going to get this training anywhere else." Second, consider video recording your trainings so they can be reused with another paraeducator. Having a paraeducator watch a video can avoid the need to arrange a common time when both the teacher and paraeducator are available. Third, when observing the paraeducator, teachers may consider multiple brief observations instead of one long observation. For example, it might be impossible for a teacher to regularly observe for an entire hour-long biology class, but it might be feasible to pop in for 5 minutes a few times each week.

Fourth, another solution for implementing observations is to have the paraeducator video record themselves in the regular education classroom so that the teacher can view the video at a convenient time. Teachers can further save time by fast forwarding the video to times that require the most involvement from the paraeducator. Fifth, coaching may be more feasible when partnering with others on the team. Often, the regular education teacher is a natural choice, given they are already present in the classroom. When the regular and special education teacher design the peer-mediated intervention plan together, the two of them can take turns observing the paraeducator and providing coaching with feedback. Related service personnel might also be well positioned to provide coaching. Often the goals being targeted by peer-mediated interventions overlap with speech or occupational therapy goals, so a transdisciplinary model of implementation is appropriate and can enhance the impact of the intervention.

Conclusion

For most teachers, implementing peer-mediated interventions is possible only with the help of paraeducators. However, the status quo for paraeducator training falls short of what is fair to students or the paraeducators themselves. The principles of effective paraeducator training outlined in this chapter are integrated into Chapters 3 through 6 of this book. Often, the success of peer-mediated interventions hinges on the degree to which paraeducators implement them as designed. Given their pivotal role in supporting inclusion, paraeducators must receive research-based training and coaching focused on peer-mediated interventions.

PART II

Selecting and Implementing Intervention Models

Part II of this book provides detailed guides for implementing four different peer-mediated interventions for students with significant disabilities. These approaches are briefly described in Table II.1. While all four models improve outcomes, each is designed to achieve somewhat different goals and to be used in different contexts, such as the classroom, the lunchroom, or at recess.

TABLE II.1 Descriptions of Practices and Examples of Good Candidates for Intervention

PRACTICE	DESCRIPTION	CANDIDATES FOR INTERVENTION
Peer Support Arrangements	One or more peers receive training and ongoing coaching to support a student with a significant disability in the regular education classroom. The goal is to increase peer interaction and classroom involvement while decreasing reliance on adult support.	• Students who rarely interact with peers in their class • Students who are largely dependent on adult support • Students who do not fully participate in class activities
Peer Network Interventions	Students meet outside of class with 2–6 peers to engage in fun activities and to build relationships. Peers receive coaching as needed to support positive interactions. Meetings might happen at lunch, during a study hall, during a club meeting time, or after school.	• Students who are not socially connected with many peers • Students who are unsuccessful in their attempts to interact with peers
FLIP Recess	Through video modeling, students are taught social skills that can be used at recess. At the same time, 3–5 peers receive training and coaching to interact and play with the student at recess.	• Students who have low rates of interaction and peer play at recess • Students who are unsuccessful in their attempts to play with peers
Peer Tutoring and Embedded Instruction	After receiving training, a peer provides brief instruction that focuses on a specific skill. This can occur at a designated time or can fit within existing classroom routines.	• Students who rarely interact with peers in their class • Students who would benefit from brief, targeted instruction

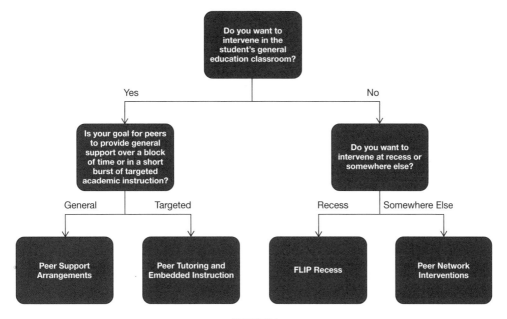

FIGURE II.1

The simple decision tree in Figure II.1 is designed to help the reader select the approach that is the best fit for a specific student and their goals. After using the decision tree to select a practice, navigate to the corresponding chapter for a step-by-step guide and resources.

3

Peer Support Arrangements: Supporting Students to Learn Together

Jose is a high school student on the autism spectrum who also has an intellectual disability. He spends most of his day in a separate special education classroom but does attend a regular education ceramics class in which he is the only student with a significant disability. A paraeducator from the special education classroom, Ms. Fernandez, accompanies Jose to the ceramics class. Ms. Fernandez and Jose sit together at a table by themselves at the back of the room. The class starts with the art teacher providing a brief lecture with instructions, then the students gather supplies and work on their projects. Jose never leaves his seat. Ms. Fernandez gathers his supplies for him and brings them to the table where they sit. The art teacher rotates around the room and talks with students to check in on their progress and to provide feedback on their projects. The teacher occasionally asks Ms. Fernandez if everything is going okay but never interacts directly with Jose. No one except for Ms. Fernandez ever talks to Jose. Despite being in the same room as his peers and a skilled art teacher, Jose's experience is no different than if he were doing ceramics with Ms. Fernandez in a separate classroom all by themselves.

For many students with significant disabilities, spending time in a general education classroom does not automatically translate into meaningful opportunities to interact with peers, learn from a content expert, or participate fully in the classroom (Carter et al., 2008). Instead, students like Jose are relegated to the periphery of the classroom, where they spend their time interacting exclusively with a paraeducator. Given little to no training on how to support students with disabilities in inclusive settings, paraeducators understandably presume that they should remain in close proximity to the student and take sole responsibility for their support (Giangreco, 2010). This style of support leads to a host of unintended consequences, including interference with peer interactions, limited interaction with the classroom teacher, unnecessary dependence on adult support, and stigmatization (Giangreco et al., 2010). This is not a failing of the paraeducator, but a systemic failure of a special education system that does not adequately prepare and supervise paraeducators to support students with disabilities in regular education classrooms. Indeed, a large body of research shows that when paraeducators are coached to deliver the right kind of support in regular education classrooms, they can contribute to substantial improvements in social and academic outcomes (Brock & Carter, 2016). The focus of this chapter is on coaching paraeducators to facilitate peer support arrangements, a proven approach for increasing social interaction and academic participation in inclusive classrooms (Brock & Huber, 2017).

What Are Peer Support Arrangements?

Peer support arrangements involve one or more peers who receive training and ongoing coaching on how to provide academic and social support to a student with a significant disability in a regular education classroom (Brock & Huber, 2017). First, the student's team develops an individualized plan for support in the regular education classroom. This plan is customized to match classroom expectations and the student's support needs. Then a teacher or paraeducator provides an initial training to one to three peers to provide them with information about the student and the strategies they can use to support the student's individualized plan. The classroom seating arrangement is altered to allow the trained peers to sit adjacent to the student and provide support. Finally, the teacher or paraeducator provides ongoing facilitation and coaching to promote positive interactions and support between the peers and the student. The facilitator strikes a balance between providing coaching when needed and fading their proximity and direct support of the student, as appropriate. A large body of research shows that peer support arrangements increase social interactions and academic engagement for students with significant disabilities (Brock & Huber, 2017). Just as importantly, this approach can have positive impacts on peers, including increased academic engagement (Jimenez et al., 2012) and more positive attitudes toward people with disabilities (Travers & Carter, 2022). While the bulk of the research on peer support arrangements has been conducted with middle and high school students, there is emerging evidence that this approach can also be effective in elementary schools (Trausch et al., 2021).

What Types of Students Benefit From Peer Support Arrangements?

Peer support arrangements are designed for students with significant disabilities who are educated for at least part of the day in a regular education classroom. The following questions are designed to identify which students would be well suited to peer support arrangements:

1. Does the student have a developmental disability (e.g., educational label of autism, intellectual disability, or multiple disabilities)?
2. Does the student have significant support needs that require curricular modifications and individualized intervention?
3. Does the student have limited or infrequent positive interactions with peers in the regular education classroom?
4. Does the student have a history that is free of aggressive behavior or violence toward peers?

If the answer to all the above questions is yes, the student is likely a good candidate for peer support arrangements.

Who Can Implement Peer Support Arrangements?

Often, the people best positioned to facilitate peer support arrangements are the paraeducators who are already tasked with supporting students with significant disabilities in regular education classrooms. Therefore, this chapter includes steps for how teachers can design peer support arrangements and effectively train and supervise paraeducators to facilitate with peers. However, it is also possible for special or regular education teachers or for a combination of staff members to work together to facilitate peer support arrangements (Carter et al., 2016). The facilitator must be someone who can be physically present in the regular education classroom during most or all the time that peer support arrangements will be implemented.

A Step-By-Step Guide for Implementing Peer Support Arrangements

This part of the chapter is a step-by-step guide to implementing peer support arrangements. It includes forms and checklists that can be reproduced, guidance for partnering with paraeducators, a vignette that illustrates what peer support arrangements look like in action, and case studies that describe common obstacles and how to overcome them.

Selecting and Recruiting Peers

Generally, two to three is the recommended number of peers to recruit for peer support arrangements. While it is technically possible to implement a peer support arrangement with only one peer, this does not allow for implementation when that peer is absent, nor does it allow for peers to rotate or share responsibility for support. At the same time, recruiting more than three peers might result in role confusion among the peers and social interactions between the peers that do not include the student with a disability.

There are a number of factors to consider when selecting peers. First, the arrangement will not be successful unless peers have good attendance and respond well to coaching from adults. Second, consider selecting peers who have good social skills and high social standing in the classroom, as this will improve their ability to model good social skills and introduce the student to other peers. Third, consider which peers have shown an interest in interacting with the student in the past and would be most likely to enjoy working closely with the student. Fourth, take into account the student's and family's personal preferences about whether the gender, racial and ethnic backgrounds, and primary language of peers match those of the student. For example, a family of a student who speaks Spanish at home might prefer that at least one of the peers is also a native Spanish speaker. Or a family may express that their Black high-school age son would prefer that at least one peer is also a Black boy.

Special education teachers, general education teachers, and paraeducators can work together to consider these factors as they nominate peers. One way for a paraeducator to invite a peer might be to say:

> You might have noticed that I sit with Evan off to the side of the room. We want Evan to have more opportunities to work more closely with his classmates, like you. We are looking for a few students who would be willing to sit next to Evan and talk with him and partner with him on work in the class. If you choose to do this, I will talk with you about Evan and teach you some ways that you can work with him. Your teacher thought that you would be really good at this and that you might enjoy it too. Does this sound like something you would like to do?

If a peer is interested, the next step is to gain permission from their parents. For a sample of what this permission form might look like, see Figure 3.5 at the end of the chapter.

Planning

When developing a peer support plan, it is best to include input from all adults who are present in the general education classroom, which often includes a general education teacher and a paraeducator. The teacher will be an expert on how their classroom is run and expectations for students. The paraeducator will be an expert in the kinds of things that the student is already able to do independently in that classroom context and areas where they need some support. Input is also needed from the special education teacher, who has expertise in designing individualized supports. It may also be helpful to include related service personnel based on the support needs of the student. For example, if a student has complex communication needs, input from a speech–language pathologist would be important. Similarly, an occupational therapist could help brainstorm ideas about how a student with a physical disability could access class materials.

A blank and an example peer support plan are provided in Figures 3.6 and 3.1. Starting a plan begins with identifying the block of time that peers will be providing support. In middle or high school, it can be easy to define that time based on the when class periods begin and end. For example, peers might provide support during a home economics class or a history class. In elementary grades, the time might be defined by an instructional block, such as reading centers, morning meeting, or science lessons. Then, consider the different types of activities that happen during this time. For example, a teacher might lecture, students might work in small groups, or students might be doing independent work. Record each of these activities as the header of a table in the peer support plan (Figure 3.2). Beneath each activity, describe general expectations for all students. For example, when a teacher is lecturing, students might be expected to listen quietly, take notes, and raise their hands to respond to the teacher or to ask questions.

FIGURE 3.1 **Example of a Peer Support Arrangements Individualized Planning Sheet**

Student Name: ___*DeSean Alexander*___

Targeted Class or Block of Day: ___*Eighth-grade Earth sciences*___

Team Members Contributing to Plan: ___*Ms. Johnson (special education teacher),*___
Mr. Evans (science teacher), Ms. Gleason (paraeducator), Ms. Fournier (speech–
language pathologist)

Instructions

Identify the types of activities that typically occur during the time that peer support arrangements will be implemented. Record each of these below in one of the "activity" lines. Complete as many pages as necessary to plan for all targeted activities.

Within each activity, list the expectations for what students should be doing during this time. Then identify what expectations the student can meet without any support, how peers might support the student to meet the expectations, and what additional support will need to be provided by an adult.

Activity: Attendance and Passing Back Work

Student expectations: Before the bell rings, students come to their tables and get out their science folder, a notebook, and a pencil. Once the bell rings, students respond by saying "here" when Mr. Evans calls their name, then the teacher selects a student to pass graded work back to the class.

What can the student do independently?	How can peers support participation?	What roles should be reserved for an adult? How can an adult support peers?
• Pull out his folder, notebook, pencil, and communication device • Chat with peers at table until the bell rings • Respond to attendance by hitting the "here" button on his communication device. • Pass papers back when selected by Mr. Evans	• Remind DeSean to get out class materials if he hasn't already gotten them out • Chat with DeSean at table until bell rings • Prompt DeSean to respond for attendance if he doesn't do it on his own • Help DeSean pass out papers by reading student names on the papers and introducing DeSean to students he does no know	• Prompt peers if needed to provide support

Activity: Lecture

Student expectations: Students are expected to listen to Mr. Evans's lecture, have their book turned to the relevant page, take notes, and raise their hands to answer questions.

What can the student do independently?	How can peers support participation?	What roles should be reserved for an adult? How can an adult support peers?
• Listen quietly to the lecture • Have his book open on the table	• Help DeSean get his book turned to the correct page • Take notes for DeSean • Summarize the key points from the lecture to DeSean	• Use positive behavior support to support DeSean's behavior • Coach peers in how to share notes and summarize in a way is accessible to DeSean • Modify or adapt upcoming assignments or activities for DeSean using guidelines provided by Ms. Johnson

Activity: Directions for Lab Activities

Student expectations: Each lab group brings materials to their table, completes the lab activity based on directions from the teacher, and answers the questions written on the board in their lab notebooks.

What can the student do independently?	How can peers support participation?	What roles should be reserved for an adult? How can an adult support peers?
• Bring the lab materials to the table • Complete parts of the lab activity with direction from peers • Copy key words from a peer's lab notebook into his own notebook	• Join DeSean's lab group • Prompt DeSean to bring the needed lab materials to the table • Find opportunities and prompt DeSean to complete parts of the lab activity • Highlight key words in their lab notebook that DeSean should copy • Prompt DeSean to copy into his lab notebook if needed	• Use positive behavior support to support DeSean's behavior • Coach peers to identify parts of the lab activity with which DeSean can be successful • Coach peers to identify the key words to highlight for DeSean

Activity: Independent Work

Student expectations: For assignments, students are expected to do their own work, although they are permitted to ask each other questions and talk about the assignment. For tests, students are expected to do their own work without any interactions.

What can the student do independently?	How can peers support participation?	What roles should be reserved for an adult? How can an adult support peers?
• Try to complete the parts of the assignment before asking for help • Ask Ms. Johnson or Mr. Evans for help if peers are still working • Ask peers for help if one of them is done working	• Make sure DeSean explains how to complete the assignment before they get started • After they are finished, compare their answer's with DeSean's and help him complete his assignment	• Use positive behavior support to support DeSean's behavior • Make modifications to assignments for DeSean as directed by Ms. Johnson • Help DeSean complete the assignment until a peer is finished with their own assignment • For tests, remove DeSean from the classroom to administer a modified test in a separate classroom

Activity: Wrap-Up and Dismissal

Student expectations: Students turn in any in-class assignments, put all other loose materials in their science folder, pack up their materials, and wait to leave until dismissed by Mr. Evans.

What can the student do independently?	How can peers support participation?	What roles should be reserved for an adult? How can an adult support peers?
• Pack up all of his materials • Walk to his locker and talk with his peers	• Prompt DeSean to pack up his materials if he has not already done so • Walk with DeSean to his locker and talk with him on the way	• Talk briefly with Mr. Evans about upcoming assignments that might need to be modified • Follow DeSean and his peers to his locker • After peers move on to their own lockers, help DeSean open locker and get out correct materials for his next class

Next, take a strength-based approach by thinking about what the student can do independently to meet expectations in each activity (Carter et al., 2015). For example, during a lecture a student might be able to listen quietly and, given a list, copy key words from the lecture down into their notebook. Then consider what supports might be appropriate for a peer to provide during the activity. For example, during a lecture a peer might sit beside the student and highlight key words in their notes for the student to copy. After the lecture, the peer might turn to the student and summarize the key points. Finally, think through what an adult would need to do during this activity. This might include roles that are inappropriate for peers, such as implementing positive behavioral supports, or it might involve coaching peers as they begin to learn and become more comfortable in their new roles. Activities during which paraeducators might not need to provide much support or coaching may be opportunities for them to work on other tasks, such as preparing materials for the general education or special education teacher, previewing the next day's lesson to brainstorm how peers could support the student, or modifying assignments as directed by a teacher. Sometimes it might be appropriate to rotate around the room to help other students while keeping an eye on the student with a disability and their peers. For examples of student, peer, and paraeducator roles during different kinds of activities, see Figure 3.1.

Peer Orientation Meeting

Once peers are selected and a plan is developed, it is time to kick off the peer support arrangement by orienting peers to their new roles. It is best to have these orientation meetings with the peers only and to not include the student with a disability. Often, the most convenient time for a meeting is during the peers' lunch, and the teacher or paraeducator can arrange for the peers to eat lunch in a classroom that is not being used. Alternatively, meetings could take place during a nonessential class activity, a study hall, or before or after school. Typically, peer orientation meetings take 30–45 minutes. If needed, an orientation meeting could be split into two shorter meetings.

The nine key components of the orientation meeting are described in the Peer Orientation Meeting Checklist in Figure 3.2 (Carter et al., 2015). Consider checking off each item during the meeting to make sure that nothing is missed. Sometimes adults think that describing the student's disability would be helpful, but this should not be done without permission from the student and their family. Typically, it is more helpful to explain the student's individual strengths and needs than to share a label like autism or intellectual disability. However, some students and families may advocate for a disability label to be shared. For example, some students and their families may see being on the autism spectrum as an integral part of their identity.

FIGURE 3.2 Peer Orientation Meeting Checklist

1. **Initial introductions (if needed)**
   - ☐ If the peers do not know you or each other, begin with introductions.
2. **Benefits for the student and the peers**
   - ☐ Explain that peer support will help the student by increasing how much they talk with their classmates, increasing their involvement in classroom activities, and helping the student to be less dependent on adults.
   - ☐ Explain that being a peer support can help them to get to know someone new they would not have otherwise interacted with and to learn more about people with disabilities.
   - ☐ Share that sometimes helping another student can help them stay more focused on what is happening in class, because they cannot help someone else unless they are listening closely.

3. **Changes to seating arrangements and groupings**
   - ☐ Explain that, in order to provide support, they will begin sitting next to the student in class and joining the same group as the student for partner or small group activities.

4. **Background about the student with a disability**
   - ☐ Describe your favorite things about the student.
   - ☐ Describe the student's interests.
   - ☐ Describe the student's style of communication.
   - ☐ Provide tips for how the peers can best communicate with the student.
   - ☐ Describe the student's strengths in the class.
   - ☐ Describe the student's support needs in the class.

5. **Review the peer support plan**
   - ☐ Provide each peer with a copy of the peer support plan
   - ☐ Explain that you and other teachers have thought through each activity in class and have considered what the student can do independently, what they can do to help, and what you will do to help.
   - ☐ Explain that this is a blueprint for how they will support the student and that as they get more experience and get more comfortable, they may come up with new ideas that can be added to the plan.
   - ☐ Walk through the plan for how peers will provide support during each activity.
   - ☐ Collect the copies of the peer support plan from the peers so they do not accidentally lose them or share them with students outside of the group.

6. **Respectful language and confidentiality**
   - ☐ Explain that it is great to talk in a positive way to others about the student with a disability or how they are working with them.
   - ☐ Explain that they need to be careful not talk about the student in a negative way, or in a way that they would not want anyone to talk about them.

7. **When to seek assistance**
   - ☐ Tell peers that they can always come to you for support or to ask questions if they are not sure what to do.
   - ☐ Explain that you will always be present in the class to keep an eye on how things are going and to help.

☐ Remind them that their first responsibility is to finish their own class-work, and they should come to you immediately if they are struggling to finish their own work.

☐ Remind peers that it is NOT their job to be the teacher, manage behavior, or do anything that they feel uncomfortable with.

8. **Invite peers to share**
   ☐ Ask each peer to share what they are most excited about.
   ☐ Ask each peer to share what they are most nervous about.

9. **Wrap-up**
   ☐ Ask peers if they have any questions for you.
   ☐ Explain when peers will begin providing support and how you will introduce them to the student with a disability.

Ongoing Facilitation and Coaching

The paraeducator begins to shift their role from directly supporting the student to indirect support through ongoing facilitation and coaching. Initially, peers often need intensive coaching to be successful. Over time, paraeducators aim to strike a balance between providing coaching when needed and backing off when the student and peers are working well together on their own.

There are six basic categories of facilitation strategies. These include prompting, reinforcing, and providing information for social interactions; and prompting, reinforcing, and providing information for academic support (Brock et al., 2019). Definitions and examples of these facilitation approaches can be found in Figure 3.3. To plan for success, brainstorm and record examples of these facilitation approaches that are specific to the student and classroom context. See Figure 3.7 at the end of the chapter for a blank facilitation planning form and Figure 3.4 for a sample of a completed form. Complete this form with the same team who created the peer support plan (e.g., general education teacher, paraeducator, special education teacher, related service personnel).

FIGURE 3.3 Strategies for Facilitating Social Interactions and Academic Support

WHAT TO SUPPORT	HOW TO SUPPORT	EXAMPLE
Social Interactions	**Prompt** the student to initiate a conversation with peers; suggest that the peers ask the student about one of their interests or experiences.	Did you know that Jolena has three cats? You should ask her about them.
	Reinforce social interactions by praising the student or peers for making an effort to talk with one another. This might happen after the conversation or class is over, so as not to impede the conversation.	I'm so impressed by how you've been talking with Kerrie and introducing her to your friends. She clearly loves talking with you and meeting new people.
	Provide information that helps peers interact with the student. This includes information about the student's communication, behavior, or interests.	When Evan rocks back and forth, that sometimes means that he is overwhelmed by the noise in the room. Maybe ask him if he wants to put on his noise-canceling headphones.
Academic Support	**Prompt** and guide the peers to support the student during classroom activities.	If you highlight key words from your notes during the lecture, I'll have Trevor copy them into his notebook.
	Reinforce peers for their efforts to support the student's participation in class.	I love how thoughtful you are being by saving for Sara the steps of the lab activity that she can be successful with.
	Provide information that helps the peers support the student's participation. This includes the student's strengths and needs, accommodations and modifications, and instructional strategies.	Robert can actually get his own materials out for class. If you just gesture to your own materials and ask Robert where his are, he will get them out on his own.

FIGURE 3.4 Sample Planning Sheet for Strategies for Facilitating Social Interactions and Academic Support

STRATEGY	WHAT COULD THIS LOOK LIKE FOR US?
Prompt social interactions	• Encourage Kerrie to greet her peers and ask them what they did last weekend. • Encourage Kerrie to share pictures from her Special Olympics bowling tournament. • Encourage peers to ask Kerrie about her pet dog. • Encourage peers to ask Kerrie about her favorite television show.
Reinforce social interactions	• Give Kerrie a thumbs up when she walks over to peers by herself and appropriately starts a conversation. • Smile at a peer when they ask Kerrie about her weekend. • After class is over, briefly let a peer know how much you appreciate their thoughtfulness and patience as they talk with Kerrie.
Provide information for social interactions	• Explain that when Kerrie rocks her body and forth, it sometimes means she is overwhelmed by the volume of sound or around her or the number of people talking at once. • Explain that Kerrie will rarely make eye contact and that they can confirm that they have her attention by saying "Give me a thumbs up if you are listening."
Prompt academic support	• Remind peers to join the same small group as Kerrie. • Remind Kerrie to sit in her new seat by her peers. • Help peers to identify jobs that Kerrie can do during a small group activity. • Remind peers to compare their work to Kerrie's after they finish an assignment. • Help peers to identify which words to highlight from their lecture notes for Kerrie to copy.
Reinforce academic support	• Tell peers, "Thanks for picking out the key words from the lecture for Kerrie to copy. This is really going to help her remember what was covered today." • Tell peers, "Kerrie loved that group activity. I am impressed how you found little jobs for her so that she could be a part of the activity.
Provide information for academic support	• Explain that asking Kerrie a question like "Do you want to pick up the materials in the front of the room?" will often result in her reflexively saying, "No way." But she is likely to respond positively to a more direct yet kind approach, like "Kerrie, please go pick up the materials from the front of the room."

Troubleshooting

Coaching peers is easy when things are going smoothly, but sometimes there are challenges. The following case studies illustrate examples of challenges and how a paraeducator can work to resolve them.

CASE STUDY 1: Kevin just wants to joke around.

PROBLEM. Ms. Marshall supports Kevin in his eighth-grade physical education (P.E.) class, and her supervising teacher has been providing training and coaching on facilitating peer support arrangements. She is excited to have just completed the peer orientation meeting and to get peer supports up and running. The first day in class, the P.E. teacher gives instructions for how to play badminton, and then directs the students to play together in small groups. Kevin and his peers make a group, collect their equipment, and find an open area of the gym where they can play. Kevin thinks the name "birdie" is a funny name for the equipment. He picks up the birdie and runs around making bird sounds, and the peers laugh at his joke. Emboldened by their response, Kevin takes his antics to a new level by flapping his arms and jumping up and down. One of the peers says to Kevin, "Kevin, would you please stop so we can start playing badminton?" But Kevin just keeps on going. The peers do not think Kevin's behavior is funny anymore and complain to Ms. Marshall that Kevin just wants to joke around.

SOLUTION. Ms. Marshall talks with the peers. First, she asks them how they would talk to a friend without a disability whom they want to stop joking around. One peer says, "I would tell them to knock it off and that it is not funny anymore." Ms. Marshall encourages the peer to communicate to Kevin in the same way. When he does, Kevin looks a little surprised and hurt but stops his antics and joins the group. After class, Ms. Marshall talks to the peers more. She thanks them for working through a tricky situation. She explains that Kevin does not get a lot of attention from peers, so when he does something that gets a laugh, he is very likely to keep doing it to try to get more laughs. She encourages them to not laugh at Kevin when he is doing something that they want him to stop and to not to be afraid to be assertive—but still kind—when asking him to stop.

OUTCOME. The next day in class they play badminton again. Immediately, Kevin grabs the birdie and starts to make bird noises. One of the peers smiles and says "Kevin, it is funny to do that once, but it is not funny when you do it over and over." Kevin smiles back and gets ready to hit the birdie over the net.

CASE STUDY 2: I'm not sure if Victoria understands any of this.

PROBLEM. Mr. Owens is a paraeducator who accompanies Victoria to a regular education fourth-grade class for a social studies block. He coaches three peers who have volunteered to support Victoria during this time. One day as the teacher lectures, a peer takes notes and highlights key words for Victoria to copy. The teacher is lecturing about the Cherokee people during colonial America, describing how they farmed maize, beans, and squash. The peer highlights the word "maize" and Victoria copies down "maze" and starts to draw a maze. The peer turns to Mr. Owens and says, "I'm not sure if Victoria understands any of this."

SOLUTION. In the moment, Mr. Owens suggests that the peer write down and highlight "maize = corn" and draw a picture of an ear of corn. After the lesson is over, Mr. Owens talks to the peer for a few minutes, away from Victoria and the other students. Mr. Owens explains that very few students always understand 100% of what is said in class. Like other students, it is okay if Victoria understands some, but not all, of what is being taught. He also compliments the peer for increasing the number of things that Victoria does understand, providing the "maize = corn" note as an example. Mr. Owens adds that there are times that he is not certain what Victoria does and does not understand but that he is confident that she is learning and belongs in the class—and he is also certain that the peer is helping Victoria learn and feel like she belongs.

OUTCOME. After their talk, the peer often asks Mr. Owens for help when Victoria does not seem to understand something. They work well as a team, and the peer seems to enjoy the challenge of thinking creatively to present information to Victoria in a way that she can understand.

CASE STUDY 3: Juliette thinks that her job is to be the teacher.

PROBLEM. The first day after orienting peers to how they will support Eduardo, Ms. Nelson is concerned by what she sees and hears. One of the peers, Juliette, thinks it is her job to manage Eduardo's behavior. When Eduardo echoes the last few words that the teacher said, Juliette turns quickly and says, "Eduardo, no talking!" Later Ms. Nelson overhears Juliette say, "Eduardo, eyes on the teacher, and hands on the desk."

SOLUTION. Ms. Nelson pulls Juliette aside where Eduardo and other students cannot hear. First, she thanks Juliette again for volunteering to support Eduardo. Next, Ms. Nelson explains that she is worried that she was not clear about the difference between a peer's role and a teacher's role. She explains again that it is an adult's job to support Eduardo to follow the classroom rules, and a peer's job is to interact with Eduardo as a friend and help him to participate in class activities. Ms. Nelson encourages Juliette to let the adults worry about Eduardo's behavior and that she can focus on her own learning and on helping Eduardo to participate. At first, Juliette is a little hurt by this feedback. She shares that she has younger siblings at home and that her mom says that she does a great job of teaching them how to behave. Ms. Nelson says that she is sure that is true, but supporting Eduardo—a classmate who is her same age—is a lot different than helping her mom with her little brothers and sisters. Ms. Nelson encourages her to think of Eduardo as a same-aged friend who sometimes needs a little extra help whom she does not ever need to tell how to behave.

OUTCOME. The next day, Juliette seems a little standoffish and unsure what to do. Ms. Nelson steps in to model how she and Eduardo can do a partner reading activity together. Ms. Nelson continues to do a lot of modeling and provides Juliette with frequent positive feedback. Over time, Juliette seems more comfortable in her new role.

Partnering With Paraeducators

For many teachers, it is not feasible to implement peer support arrangements alone. Often, the success of peer support arrangements hinges on partnering with a paraeducator who is already supporting the student in the regular education classroom. There are proven training and supervision strategies that set paraeducators up to be successful (Brock & Anderson, 2021). These include defining roles, explaining how the intervention will benefit the student, walking through a checklist of steps, modeling the steps, and observing and providing feedback. This section describes how to apply each of these strategies to peer support arrangements.

Define Roles

It is the teacher's responsibility to plan and design peer support arrangements. This means the teacher is responsible for identifying students who would benefit from the intervention, identifying peers who will provide support, and writing the peer support plan. At the same time, it is appropriate and prudent for teachers to solicit input from paraeducators when identifying peers and writing the peer support plan. Given the time they have spent in the regular education classroom with students, paraeducators are often well positioned to provide suggestions about potential peers or to describe the student's support needs within the classroom routines. Appropriate roles for paraeducators include implementing initial peer training, coaching peers in the classroom, and providing direct support to the student as specified in the peer support plan. Teachers should be explicit about which of these roles they are asking paraeducators to do.

Talk About the Benefits for the Student

Share that peer support arrangements have the potential to increase the student's interactions with peers, increase the number of peers that the student knows in the classroom, increase the student's involvement in classroom activities, and decrease their dependence on adult support.

Walk Through the Checklist

Provide the paraeducator with checklists and planning sheets that correspond with their responsibilities. For example, Figure 3.2 describes steps for conducting initial peer training, Figure 3.1 provides a sample peer support plan, and Figure 3.4 provides a sample plan for coaching peers. Explain each step or strategy, and check for understanding with the paraeducator.

Model the Steps

Paraeducators are most likely to implement the steps as designed if they observe a teacher do them first. With the paraeducator observing, implement the initial training and model how to coach peers in the classroom. Paraeducators can be active observers by following along with the implementation checklists and planning sheets from Figures 3.1, 3.2, or 3.4 as they observe.

Observe and Provide Feedback

Observe the paraeducator when they implement their first initial peer training, when they provide coaching for the first time at recess, and then intermittently over time. Use the implementation checklists and planning sheets as guides for supporting the paraeducator. For the initial peer training, the implementation checklist provides a sequential list of straightforward steps. If the paraeducator misses one of the steps, the teacher can step in to help make sure that it gets covered. If the problem was just forgetting to do the step, the teacher might just point to the step to remind the paraeducator. If the paraeducator is unsure what to do, the teacher might remodel the implementation of that step.

Helping a paraeducator provide coaching can be more challenging. Although there are strategies detailed in Figure 3.3, there are also elements of judgement and improvisation about when and how to provide support based on individual students and situations. For example, paraeducators must be able to recognize when things are going well, such that they should step back, and which challenges require that they step in. In addition, paraeducators will need to make judgments about how much structure is required when providing support. Supporting paraeducators with these skills is not as simple as pointing out a missed step on a checklist and often will require more dialogue. One approach is for teachers to talk about what they are observing and why and how they are deciding to intervene based on what they see. Sharing their decision-making process out loud in real-time can help the paraeducator understand how to make similar decisions in the future. It may also be helpful to talk through the case studies in this chapter that illustrate how to troubleshoot when peers are hesitant, frustrated, or unsure what to do.

Peer Support Arrangements in Action

The following vignette, a composite of real experiences, illustrates what peer support arrangements look like in action. At the beginning of this chapter you read about Jose, a high school student with intellectual disability who spent ceramics classes at a separate table with Ms. Fernandez, a paraeducator. Jose never got up from the table and depended on the paraeducator to get class materials for him. Below you'll read about how Jose's teacher used peer support arrangements to promote more meaningful inclusion for Jose and to decrease his reliance on adult support.

Jose's special education teacher, Ms. Davis, goes to a special education conference where she learns about an approach called peer support arrangements. Ms. Davis gets excited when she hears that peer support arrangements can offer a way to increase peer interactions and participation in class activities. Ms. Davis has always been an advocate for inclusion. She pushes hard at her school to make sure her students have opportunities to go to regular education classrooms. Now, peer support arrangements could better enable her students to fully experience the social and academic benefits of inclusion.

Ms. Davis sets up a meeting with Ms. Fernandez, Mr. Miller (the art teacher), and Ms. Seward (the speech–language pathologist). Ms. Davis shares that the reason she brought them together was to try to a new approach with Jose called peer support arrangements. Together, they start to make a peer support plan. First, Mr. Miller and Ms. Fernandez take the lead, as the team lists the type of activities that typically happen in ceramics class. Ms. Davis asks them what tasks Jose can already do by himself. She is surprised to learn that Ms. Fernandez has been getting Jose's materials for him and proposes that this might be an example of something Jose can do for himself in the future. Next, the team thinks about the role that peers might play. Mr. Miller says that most class projects are very open-ended, so there is a lot of flexibility in how Jose completes his work. Ms. Fernandez agrees and shares that she spends much of her time encouraging Jose, complimenting his work, and chatting with him. The team agrees that these are all things that peers would be able to do, and they add them to the support plan. Ms. Seward provides some suggestions for helping the peers communicate with Jose, who uses augmentative and alternative communication (AAC). She suggests that peers be coached to wait several seconds for Jose to respond and to look for subtle nonverbal communications, like facial expressions. Then, the team agrees that Ms. Fernandez's role should include coaching the peers and stepping in as needed with positive behavioral supports. To give Ms. Fernandez some ideas about how to coach peers, the team also fills out a facilitation planning sheet. Finally, the team works together to nominate peers who might excel at providing support. They think about which students have regular attendance, good social skills, and might like to interact more with Jose. They also consider that Jose's family communicated a preference for them to select male students and for at least one of the peers to speak Spanish—the language that they speak to Jose at home.

The next day in class, Ms. Fernandez invites each nominated peer to be a peer support for Jose and gives each a permission slip for their family to sign. All the permission forms come back within a few days, and Ms. Fernandez arranges for orientation training to take place the next week during their lunch period in a classroom that is unused at that time. In the meantime, Ms. Davis meets with Ms. Fernandez to explain how to lead the orientation meeting and how to provide facilitation and coaching. Ms. Davis goes through the orientation checklist and talks through each step. She also goes through the categories of facilitation strategies and reviews the ideas they brainstormed on the planning sheet. Ms. Davis says that she will lead the orientation meeting, since Ms. Fernandez has not seen one done before, but that Ms. Fernandez is welcome to jump in and will lead the next one on her own.

At the orientation meeting, the peers seem excited to get started. The next day in class, Ms. Davis stops in. She compliments Ms. Fernandez for how well things are going and models a couple of the facilitation strategies. Over the next few weeks, three changes occur. First, Jose begins to do things for himself that Ms. Fernandez used to do for him. He gets his own supplies at the beginning of class and cleans and puts them away at the end of class. Second, Jose smiles a lot more in class. He is not always able to use his AAC device because his hands are busy molding clay, but his nods and smiles show his peers that he loves sitting with them and being included in their conversations. Third, Ms. Fernandez begins to fade her support from Jose and to take on other roles in the classroom. She sits at an adjacent table where she can still hear when her help is needed. She spends most of her time prepping materials for Ms. Davis or Mr. Miller. At the end of class, one of the peers walks Jose to the special education classroom while Ms. Davis follows from a distance.

Ms. Davis tells Ms. Fernandez that she is thrilled with how well things are going. Ms. Fernandez comments that she loves facilitating peer support arrangements and that she appreciates Ms. Davis mentoring her to support Jose in a new way. The two of them begin to discuss other students who might be good candidates for peer support arrangements.

Conclusion

With peer support arrangements, paraeducators shift away from sitting near the student and supporting them directly and instead coach peers to provide more natural support. This approach benefits students with increased opportunities to observe and practice social and communication skills, increased engagement in class activities, and decreased dependence on adults. Peers can also benefit from increased engagement in class activities, learning new skills, and becoming more comfortable interacting with people who have disabilities. Successful implementation requires special education teachers, general education teachers, and paraeducators to work together as a team. Together, they can enable students with significant disabilities to realize the full benefits of inclusion.

FIGURE 3.5 Sample Permission Form for Families of Peers Providing Support

Dear Parents and Families,

One of your child's teachers has recommended your child to be a peer partner with a student in their classroom who has a disability. If your child participates, your child and two other peers in the class would take turns sitting with the student during their ceramics class. They would talk with the student and work together on projects. An adult would meet with your child and the other two peers to provide guidance about how to communicate and work with the student. The same adult will supervise and support them work as they work together. Your child was recommended because they have good social skills and show kindness and patience with others.

Please send this form to your child's teacher to let us know if it is okay with you for your child to participate as a peer partner.

Check one:

_____ **Yes**, I give permission for my child to be a peer partner in ceramics class.

_____ **No**, I do not give my permission for my child to be a peer partner in ceramics class.

Your Signature _____ Date _____

FIGURE 3.6 Blank Peer Support Arrangements Individualized Planning Sheet

Student Name _____

Targeted Class or Block of Day _____

Team Members Contributing to Plan _____

Instructions

1. Identify the types of activities that typically occur during the time that peer support arrangements will be implemented. Record each of these below in one of the "activity" lines. Complete as many pages as necessary to plan for all targeted activities.

2. Within each activity, list the expectations for students. Then identify what expectations the student can meet without any support, how peers might support the student to meet the expectations, and what additional support will need to be provided by an adult.

Activity:		
Student expectations:		
What can the student do independently?	How can peers support participation?	What roles should be reserved for an adult? How can an adult support peers?

continues

Note: This page should be copied as many times as needed to include all activities.

FIGURE 3.7 Blank Planning Sheet for Strategies for Facilitating Social Interactions and Academic Support

STRATEGY	WHAT COULD THIS LOOK LIKE FOR US?
Prompt social interactions	
Reinforce social interactions	
Provide information for social interactions	
Prompt academic support	
Reinforce academic support	
Provide information for academic support	

4

Peer Network Interventions:
Building Social Connections Outside of Class

Sierra is a middle school student with cerebral palsy. She speaks a few words, but primarily communicates by selecting words and phrases on a program on her tablet computer. Sierra receives special education services under the disability category of multiple disabilities. It is easy to predict where Sierra will be every day at lunch. She always sits with other students with disabilities and Ms. Johnson, a paraeducator who provides her with one-to-one support, at a table in the back of the cafeteria. Sierra has never really made a choice about where to sit. On the first day of junior high, Ms. Johnson helped Sierra and other students with disabilities navigate the lunch line, then led them all to the same table. There was no intentional decision to sit away from other students; this was just the most convenient option at the time, and the routine stuck. While students at other tables talk and joke with friends, Sierra's table is mostly quiet, except for Ms. Johnson occasionally chatting with one of the students or offering help.

The most social times of a student's day are usually not in the classroom. More often, they occur in lunchroom, in the hallway, during extracurricular activities and clubs, or at after-school events. Many students with significant disabilities have very limited access to these social environments. Students with significant disabilities sometimes eat lunch in a special education classroom, navigate the hallways at a different time than other students, and participate only in extracurricular activities designed exclusively for people with disabilities (Herbert et al., 2020). Even when students with disabilities are in the same room as their peers, there are still barriers to peer interactions. Some barriers inadvertently stem from actions of well-meaning school staff (Giangreco et al., 2010). In Sierra's case, a paraeducator who was trying to help students have a smooth first experience in the lunch line unintentionally established a routine where students with disabilities segregated themselves at a separate lunch table. Similarly, a teacher or paraeducator might walk closely beside a student during transitions between classes, making it less likely that a peer will greet or interact with the student. These support behaviors inadvertently exacerbate the challenges that students with significant disabilities already face due to deficits in social skills and communication.

What Are Peer Network Interventions?

Peer network interventions are designed to overcome the barriers that make it challenging for students with significant disabilities to build friendships with peers. These interventions involve recruiting peers who would enjoy getting to know the student better, organizing and facilitating regular opportunities for interaction, and encouraging peers to make contact with the student at other times during and after school (Hochman et al., 2015). A facilitator organizes peer network meetings at times that make sense, given the student's age and context. For example, high school students might meet during a shared study hall, elementary students might meet during indoor recess, and middle school students might meet over lunch.

Peer network interventions provide new opportunities to make social connections that might develop into friendships. While friendships often emerge, this outcome cannot be guaranteed. Like when any two people meet for the first time, a friendship only emerges when both people enjoy one another's company and continue to seek each other out. Students without disabilities naturally have many opportunities to interact with classmates, gauge how much they enjoy these interactions, and decide whether they would like to be friends. Peer network interventions simply extend these same opportunities to students with significant disabilities.

What Types of Students Benefit From Peer Network Interventions?

Peer network interventions are designed to improve social connections for students with significant disabilities who have very few social connections with students without disabilities. The following questions are designed to identify students who would be a good fit for peer network interventions:

1. Does the student have a developmental disability (e.g., educational label of autism, intellectual disability, or multiple disabilities)?
2. Does the student have significant support needs that require curricular modifications and individualized intervention?
3. Does the student rarely interact with peers without disabilities, even when they are in the same physical space?

If the answer to all the above questions is yes, the student is likely a good candidate for peer network intervention.

Who Can Implement Peer Network Interventions?

Peer network interventions can be implemented by any school staff who are available during the targeted meeting time (e.g., lunch, study hall, club meeting time). When possible, it is ideal to select someone who is already familiar with the student with a disability and is skilled in facilitating socialization between students. In research studies, many kinds of school staff have been effective facilitators, including school counselors, special education teachers, general education teachers, paraeducators, and school administrators (Asmus et al., 2017).

A Step-By-Step Guide for Implementing Peer Network Interventions

This part of the chapter is a step-by-step guide for implementing peer network interventions. It includes forms and checklists that can be reproduced, guidance for partnering with paraeducators, a vignette that illustrates what peer network interventions look like in action, and case studies that describe common obstacles and how to overcome them.

Selecting and Recruiting Peers

Two to six peers will need to be selected. There are four criteria for selecting peers. First, it is critical to select peers who would be able to consistently attend network meetings at the targeted time. This might be a shared lunch, study hall, club meeting time, or a time after school. Second, when possible, it can be helpful to select peers who share common interests with the student with a disability. This is especially helpful when a student tends to talk only about a small number of special interests. Third, based on student and family preferences, consider identifying peers that match the student's gender and racial or ethnic group. The importance of these characteristics may change based on the student's age and context. For example, matching a boy with mostly girl peers might work fine for first graders but might be problematic for high school students. It is important to not make assumptions about a student's or family's desire to include peers who match the student's racial or ethnic group and to instead have a conversation with the student and family. Fourth, pick peers who will model good social skills for the student.

There are several avenues for identifying peers who meet these criteria. First, ask the student themselves if there are peers that they would like to hang out with and get to know better. Second, talk with adults who know potential peers well, such as general education teachers or paraeducators. Third, conduct an informal class-wide survey to identify peers who are available at the same time and share some of the student's interests. Sometimes it can be helpful to ask a peer who has agreed to participate if they have friends who might also like to be involved.

Inviting peers involves asking them if they would enjoy hanging out with and getting to know the student with a disability. Be sure to explain to peers when and how often the peer network will meet so that they understand what they are agreeing to. In addition, secure permission from parents before moving forward. See Figure 4.1 for a sample permission form for parents of prospective peers.

FIGURE 4.1 Sample Permission Form for Families of Peers

Dear Parent,

I am a special education teacher at your child's school, and I am working to create opportunities for students with and without disabilities to get to know each other better. When I spoke with your child's teacher, they recommended your child as someone who might enjoy having an opportunity to interact with a student with a disability.

With your permission, I would like to set up times for your child and other students with and without disabilities to eat lunch together at school. An adult would help introduce the students to one another and coach your child in some simple strategies to help them interact with the student who has a disability. The goal is for this to be a fun time for all involved.

Please complete the form below to let me know if it would be okay with you if your child participates in this lunch group.

_____ **Yes**, I give my permission for my child to participate in a lunch group focused on supporting opportunities for students with and without disabilities to interact.

_____ **No**, I do not want my child to participate in the lunch group.

Child's Name _____

Parent Signature _____ Date _____

Planning

Three kinds of planning can help ensure a successful kick-off meeting. These include planning how the student will share background information about themselves, identifying peer strategies that could promote successful interactions, and brainstorming a list of fun activities that would be feasible at meetings.

Record Background Information About the Student. Often a student with a significant disability could benefit from support when introducing themselves and talking about themselves. This involves thinking through what the student might want to share about themselves and what supports they might need to do so. The blank form in Figure 4.4 can serve as a guide for collecting information a student might want to share about themselves. This type of form can be completed in advance with the student and others who know the student well, such as a parent or sibling.

After recording this information, think about how the student would be able to share this information as independently as possible. Some students might be able to speak about themselves with intermittent prompting from an adult. Other students might benefit from prerecording information onto an AAC device. In other cases, it might be helpful for the student to share about themselves by showing photographs. For example, a student might show pictures of themselves with their family, with a pet, doing something they enjoy outside of school, and something they enjoy talking about. Photographs can enable students with complex communication needs to get ideas across that would be very challenging with only their AAC device. Photographs can also naturally lead to follow-up questions from peers (Light & McNaughton, 2012).

Identify Peer Strategies to Promote Successful Interactions. In many cases, limited social interactions between students with significant disabilities and their peers stem from barriers such as communication challenges or behaviors that are misunderstood. Fortunately, it is possible to reduce these barriers by proactively coaching peers to use interaction strategies (Biggs et al., 2018). Strategies should be tailored to addressing potential barriers based on the individual student and situation. For example, some students might engage in unusual or stereotypical behavior that is confusing or intimidating to peers. This might include hand flapping, body rocking, or intense staring. Overcoming these barriers involves supporting peers in understanding and responding to the behavior. In the case of hand flapping, a facilitator might explain that this behavior could mean more than one thing. Sometimes it might indicate the student is excited, and other times it might mean the volume of noise in the room is uncomfortable and overwhelming. Peers might first consider whether it is more likely the student is excited or overwhelmed based on the situation, and then confirm by asking the student. If the student is overwhelmed, the peers might try talking more softly or taking turns, talking one at a time.

Another barrier might be that a student engages in an undesirable or unwanted behavior and peers are unsure what to do. In this situation, peers need a proactive strategy to reduce the likelihood of the behavior, a reactive strategy if the behavior happens, and a plan to seek out the facilitator if the behavior persists. For example, some students might grab and eat any food that is close to them, even if it is on someone else's plate. This can be a significant barrier if a peer network meets during lunch. A proactive strategy would be to coach peers to maintain distance from the student and to position their food so that it would be difficult for the student to reach. If the student still grabs for their food, a response might be to tell the student, "I want to sit with you, but I really don't like it when you take my food," and to move further away from the student. If the behavior persists, the peers would be instructed to ask the facilitator for help.

A different barrier might involve a student who wants to talk only about a narrow topic that is not interesting to peers. For example, a student might want to talk only about trains, a television show, a sports team, or a comic book character. An adult facilitator might coach peers to decide whether they want to talk about the student's interest and how to redirect the student to a common experience or shared interest if they do not. For example, the facilitator might model a statement like, "I am impressed by how much you know about trains, but I am ready to talk about something different. We both have dogs—does yours do any tricks?"

These and other examples of strategies that address barriers to communication are described in Figure 4.2. Typically, it is better to select only one or two strategies. This increases the likelihood that peers will remember the strategies and apply them well.

FIGURE 4.2 Examples of Barriers to Communication and Strategies to Address Them

BARRIER TO COMMUNICATION	STRATEGY
Unusual or stereotypical behavior is confusing or intimidating to peers	Explain to the peers how they might interpret and respond to the behavior
Student struggles to keep up with the pace of the conversation	Peers wait at least 5 seconds for a response
Peers are unsure what a student said or communicated	Peers may ask student to repeat or may ask a clarifying question
Student focuses conversation on a restricted interest that is not interesting to peers	Peers redirect conversation to a shared experience or interest

continues

Student engages in unwanted or undesirable behavior	Peers use a proactive strategy to reduce the likelihood of behavior occurring, a reactive strategy when the behavior occurs, and seek adult help if the behavior persists
Peers are unsure how to communicate with a student who communicates using an AAC device	With the student's permission, have both the peers and the student communicate back and forth using the device

Note: Subsets of these strategies are described in Biggs et al., 2018 and Herbert et al., 2020.

Make a List of Activities. The last step of planning is making a list of activities that would be feasible and enjoyed by the student and peers. The nature of these activities is dependent on the age and interests of the students, the materials that are available at the school, and the context of the peer network meetings. For example, elementary students who have finished eating during a lunch meeting might enjoy drawing together on a large piece of butcher block paper, playing a card game, or building with magnetic blocks. Middle school students meeting during a study hall might enjoy playing Mad Libs, taking group selfies and applying photo filters, or playing a pop trivia game. This list of activities will be a resource that the facilitator can draw from as they prepare for upcoming network meetings. Over time, the student and peers may gravitate toward certain types of activities or propose new activities that were not on the original list.

Kickoff Meeting

The kickoff meeting is an opportunity to get the peer network off to a positive start. The steps for the kickoff meeting are described in Figure 4.3.

FIGURE 4.3 Implementation Checklist for Kickoff Network Meeting

☐ **Introduce the student and peers to each other** if they do not already know each other well.

☐ **Explain the purpose of the network,** which is to have fun and build new friendships.

☐ **Support the student and peers to share about themselves.** Have the student and peers each take a turn sharing about themselves, their interests, and their family. Support the student as specified in the plan. If the student has complex communication challenges, this might involve helping the student to share information that is preprogrammed into their AAC device or sharing pictures from a computer or a photo book.

☐ **Explain how often the network will meet and what they will do.** Tell the student and peers how many times they will be meeting each week. Share examples of activities they will be doing from the activity list.

☐ **Introduce strategies to support positive interactions.** Explain to the peers that there are some things they will need to know in order to be a good friend to the student with a disability. Describe each potential barrier to communication, the strategy designed to address it, and provide examples of what the strategy would look like in action.

☐ **If time permits, do an interactive activity.** Choose, or have the students and peers choose, one of the activities from the list. Support them to interact with one another and engage with the activity in the remaining time.

☐ **Wrap up and discuss next steps.** Remind the student and peers of when the next meeting will be. Have each peer set a goal for how they will communicate with the student at least once before the next meeting.

Regular Meetings

Subsequent meetings are less structured and should involve less direction from the facilitator. First, the facilitator should ensure they, the student, or the peers plan and bring materials for an activity. The activity list made by the facilitator in the planning stage can be a starting place. For elementary-age students, the facilitator may always need to plan and bring materials for an activity. Middle and high school students might take more ownership in planning and bringing materials. Second, the facilitator should support positive interactions during the activity as needed. Sometimes the peers and student will need help to get a conversation going or to figure out how best to include the student in an activity. Third, the facilitator should look for opportunities to fade their proximity and support when possible. The end goal is for the student and peers to have natural interactions with one another. So when things are going well, the facilitator can supervise from a distance. Fourth, wrap-up and discuss next steps. Just as in the kickoff meeting, this involves reminding the students and peers of when the next network meeting will be, and having the peers set goals for how they will communicate with the student between meetings.

Troubleshooting

Sometimes peer network interventions go very smoothly, but other times there are challenges. This section provides three case examples of how facilitators worked through challenges.

CASE STUDY 1: Ricardo's texting is out of control.

PROBLEM. Mr. Edwards has been facilitating a peer network for Ricardo, a middle school student with intellectual disability. At first, the peer network seems to be going great. Ricardo and his peers love to play board games and talk about sports and pop culture. But then one of the peers asks to talk privately with Mr. Edwards. The peer explains that he started to keep in touch with Ricardo in between meetings by texting. At first it was fun, but then Ricardo started texting a lot—often the same repetitive messages, like "What's up?" and "What are you doing?" The peer shows his phone to Mr. Edwards, who is shocked to see that Ricardo is sending the peer about fifty texts a day. The peer shares that they are worried because they do not want to ignore Ricardo, but that it is difficult to even know how to respond to so many similar messages.

SOLUTION. First, Mr. Edwards thanks the peer for sharing this with him. Mr. Edwards explains that Ricardo does not have a lot of friends and has not really gotten the hang of how often it makes sense to send text messages. They discuss about how many text message exchanges would be enjoyable. Next, they talk with Ricardo together. With Mr. Edward's support, the peer tells Ricardo that he likes to text with him but that so many text messages is too much. The peer explains to Ricardo that he would like to set a limit of Ricardo sending up to five text messages each day. The peer will respond to those five text messages, but after that he will stop until the next day. Mr. Edwards tells Ricardo that part of being a good friend is listening to your friend and respecting how they want to interact. Mr. Edward tells Ricardo that there is a "just right" amount of texting, and texting too much will make it less likely that his friends will respond.

OUTCOME. After talking with the peer and Mr. Edwards, Ricardo sends his friend exactly five texts each day. The peer is relieved with the more manageable text conversations, and in other situations he is more confident letting Ricardo know when something makes him uncomfortable.

CASE STUDY 2: Peter only wants to talk about Pokémon.

PROBLEM. Peter's social network has been going great. The facilitator, Ms. Ford, found three peers that shared Peter's common interest in Pokémon, and Peter loves talking to them about it. But after several weeks, the peers grow exhausted of talking about Pokémon. "I never thought I would say this, but talking this much about Pokémon is starting to drive me crazy," one peer tells Ms. Ford. The other two peers feel the same way.

SOLUTION. Ms. Ford talks with the three peers and asks them if they want to completely stop talking about Pokémon or if they just want to talk about it less. They all agree that they just want to talk about it less. Ms. Ford proposes that the first five minutes of lunch will be "Pokémon time." They will set a timer, and there will be a picture on laminated card of a Pokémon character. After five minutes when the timer rings, they will flip the picture upside down and Pokémon time will be over. Ms. Ford talks with Peter separately to explain the new plan. Ms. Ford also gives the peers a list of other things that Peter might enjoy talking about, including video games, ninjas, and his dog. She tells them that if Peter talks about Pokémon after the Pokémon time is over, it is okay to tell him, "Pokémon time is over," and redirect the conversation.

OUTCOME. At first, Peter is very resistant to the new plan. He does not understand why anyone would want to spend less time talking about Pokémon. Ms. Ford explains that being a good friend means that he gets to decide what they talk about some of the time but not all the time. Being a good friend means sometimes letting his friends decide what to do or talk about. Peter reluctantly falls in with the new plan, although he occasionally needs a reminder that Pokémon time is over. The peers are relieved to not be talking only about Pokémon, and one of them thanks Ms. Ford for helping them figure out a solution.

CASE STUDY 3: We have run out of things to talk about.

PROBLEM. Candace's social network never really took off. Her middle school peers still seem puzzled how to communicate with someone who uses an AAC device. They try to steer the conversation to topics that they know Candace can communicate about with her AAC device. This makes conversations feel forced and robotic. Candace has only a few conversational messages programmed into her device, so her participation is limited and repetitive. One of the peers tells the facilitator, Ms. Baez, that they have run out of things to talk about.

SOLUTION. Ms. Baez talks with the peers and proposes two solutions. First, she acknowledges that the AAC device does not have all the words and messages that Candace needs. She asks the peers to make a list of ten things that they want to talk about that are missing from Candace's device. Ms. Baez shares this list with Candace's special education teacher, who works with a speech–language pathologist to program in new vocabulary into the AAC device. Second, Ms. Baez explains that they don't have to only talk about topics that are on Candace's device. They are welcome to talk about anything that they would normally talk about with friends. She explains that Candace can communicate in other ways such as smiling or shaking her head. Also, Candace enjoys it when they talk with her about things they like or are doing. She cares more about feeling like they are including her and acknowledging her than always having an opportunity to use her AAC device.

OUTCOME. The network meetings start to feel much more relaxed and fun. The peers grow increasingly comfortable talking to Candace without worrying so much about whether she has words to contribute from her AAC device. Candace's smile shows that she enjoys when her new friends talk with her, even if she doesn't always have the words she would need to talk back. Occasionally, Candace surprises the peers by bringing up a new topic of conversation that they did not know was programmed into her AAC device. Ms. Baez and the peers agree to keep making new lists of words and topics to add to Candace's device.

Partnering With Paraeducators

In many situations, it is not feasible for one teacher to maintain implementation of a peer network intervention. Many different adults at a school could serve as a facilitator, including school counselors, administrators, paraeducators, or other teachers. Often, it is most feasible to partner with a paraeducator who is already supporting a student during lunch, at a study hall, or during a high school period designated for club meetings. This section focuses on how to leverage proven training and supervision strategies that set paraeducators up for success (Brock & Anderson, 2021). These include defining roles, explaining how the intervention will benefit the student, walking through a checklist of steps, modeling the steps, and observing and providing feedback. This section describes what each of these strategies looks like in the context of peer network interventions.

Define Roles

It is the teacher's responsibility to plan and design peer network interventions. This means the teacher is responsible for identifying students who would benefit from the intervention, identifying peers who will provide support, and designing peer strategies to promote successful interactions. Teachers might solicit input from paraeducators when identifying peers—especially if they are already familiar with peers who have shown interest in the student during lunch. Appropriate roles for paraeducators include implementing initial peer training, completing the student background sheet (with input from the student, their family, and the teacher), leading peer network meetings, and brainstorming and organizing activities for the meetings. Teachers should be explicit about which of these roles they are asking paraeducators to play.

Talk About the Benefits for the Student

Share that peer network interventions remove barriers that keep students with significant disabilities from having meaningful interactions with peers and might provide opportunities to build friendships.

Walk Through the Checklist

Provide the paraeducator with the initial meeting checklist in Figure 4.3. Describe each step, and check for understanding with the paraeducator. In addition, share peer strategies that have been designed to promote interactions (see Figure 4.2).

Model the Steps

Paraeducators are most likely to implement the steps as designed if they have observed a teacher do it first. With the paraeducator observing, lead the first network meeting and model how to coach peers to use the strategies. Paraeducators can be active observers by following along with the checklist in Figure 4.3.

Observe and Provide Feedback

Observe the paraeducator when they implement their first network meeting and then intermittently over time. Because network meetings are somewhat unstructured, there are not sequential steps that the paraeducator must follow. Instead, look for the degree to which the student and peers are engaging in positive, reciprocal interactions. Provide positive feedback about how the paraeducator is supporting things to go well, and provide constructive feedback about what they could do differently when the quality of interactions could be improved. If a paraeducator does not understand a suggestion, offer to model it for them during a network meeting.

Peer Network Intervention in Action

At the beginning of this chapter you read about Sierra, a middle school student who sat at a lunch table with a paraeducator (Ms. Johnson) and other students with significant disabilities. Below you'll read how Sierra's teacher used a peer network intervention to transform lunch into a meaningful opportunity for socialization and building relationships with peers.

Ms. Johnson and Sierra's teacher, Ms. Young, attend a district-wide professional development day where the presenter talks about peer network interventions. The presenter explains that peer network interventions can help students build a network of friends that they interact with both during and after the school day. She explains that lunch is an ideal time to establish peer network meetings and for the students and peers to get to know each other. Ms. Young and Ms. Johnson exchange a stunned look. It had never occurred to them that lunch could be an opportunity to support the social development of their students, but they are open to giving it a try.

The next day, Ms. Young talks with Ms. Johnson about peers that have had positive interactions with Sierra or have worked well with Sierra in classes. She also asks Sierra if there are any peers that she would like to spend more time with. She talks one-on-one with each of the peers that Ms. Johnson and Sierra suggest and finds four girls who say they would love to eat lunch with Sierra two times each week. Ms. Johnson sends permission forms home with the girls, and they bring them back with parent signatures the next day.

Since Ms. Johnson has never implemented a kickoff meeting before, Ms. Young walks her through all the steps. Ms. Young explains that she will lead Sierra's kickoff meeting to model all the steps. Then Ms. Johnson will be ready to lead the rest of Sierra's network meetings as well as kickoff meetings for other students in the future. Ms. Young asks Sierra's family to email digital pictures of her, her interests, her family, and her pets. Ms. Young loads the pictures onto Sierra's tablet computer, and Ms. Johnson helps Sierra practice accessing and sharing the pictures. Ms. Young and Ms. Johnson work together to make a list of activities that might be fun for the girls.

At the kickoff meeting, Ms. Young introduces all the girls to one another and explains that the purpose of the network is to have fun and build new friendships. Next each girl shares a little bit about herself. When it is Sierra's turn, she confidently shows the pictures of herself and her interests just like she practiced with Ms. Johnson. The peers talk about the pictures and ask Sierra questions. Sometimes Sierra answers by herself, and other times Ms. Johnson needs to help Sierra navigate to the right page on her AAC device. Ms. Young explains that the girls will eat lunch and play games together two times each week. One peer asks if they can have lunch with Sierra more often, and Ms. Young says that they are welcome to eat lunch with Sierra or whomever they want on the other three days. Next, Ms. Young models the strategy of wait time. She explains that it takes time for Sierra to think about what has been said, plan what she wants to say, and then find her words on her computer. This means that often she will not answer right away and that sometimes peers may need to wait as long as five seconds for Sierra to start to use her computer to find her words. By this time, the girls have finished eating and there are about five minutes left in the lunch period. Ms. Young pulls out a Mad Libs book and a pencil, and the girls have fun reading the silly stories that they make together. As they wrap up, Ms. Young asks the peers to set goals for how they will try to keep in touch with Sierra before the next meeting. Two peers say they will stop and talk to Sierra at her locker during one of the passing periods. Another says that she will stop by Sierra's lunch table for a few minutes to chat with her. The fourth peer says she will stop by the special education classroom to say hi on her way to homeroom in the morning.

Ms. Johnson runs the next meeting by herself. The girls chat while they eat, and then Ms. Johnson helps them play a gameshow-style pop trivia game on Sierra's computer. Sierra navigates the computer and holds it up so that the group can read the questions and answer choices. Ms. Young pops in for the last few minutes to see how things are going. Ms. Johnson asks the girls if they have ideas for what they want to do for fun at meetings in the future. They ask if they can play the trivia game again and also suggest several ideas that Ms. Johnson had not thought of. They keep the same goals for how they will keep in touch with Sierra between meetings. After the meeting, Ms. Young checks in with Ms. Johnson to see how it went. They both agree that things are going great. Ms. Young says she will try to pop in for a few minutes each week and would also love to hear updates from Ms. Johnson on other days.

Over time, peers who were not part of the original group come to join the peer network meetings. Ms. Johnson is unsure if this is okay, but Ms. Young assures her this is a wonderful outcome, as long as Sierra is still a part of the conversation and activities. With encouragement from

Ms. Young, Ms. Johnson moves from sitting at the same table as Sierra and her peers to an adjacent table by herself. At first Sierra seems a little anxious without Ms. Young close by, but over time she grows more confident about sitting only with her peers.

One day during lunch one of the peers asks Sierra if she would like to go together to watch their high school basketball team play. Sierra excitedly says yes, and Ms. Young connects the peer with Sierra's mom so they can work out details. Sierra's mom is ecstatic. This is the first time that Sierra has ever been invited by another student to do anything together outside of school. Ms. Johnson continues to communicate regularly with Ms. Young about how the social network is going, and they excitedly discuss setting up similar interventions for other students.

Conclusion

With peer network interventions, teachers can build meaningful opportunities for students with significant disabilities to socialize and build friendships. These flexible interventions can take place at lunch, after school, during a study hall, or during a club meeting time. The role of a facilitator—often a paraeducator—is key to the peer network's success. The facilitator's goal is to strike a balance between providing support, when needed, and fading their proximity and support to make way for more natural interactions. Training and feedback from teachers are crucial to helping paraeducators strike this balance.

FIGURE 4.4 Blank Background Sheet

Does the student have siblings or pets at home?

What does the student like to do outside of school?

What does the student like to talk about?

What kinds of games does the student enjoy playing?

If someone were talking with the student for the first time, what would they need to understand about the student's communication?

What is the best way to communicate with the student outside of school?

5

FLIP Recess: Building Social Skills and Friendships on the Playground

Jeremy—a second-grader on the autism spectrum and with intellectual disability—spends most of recess walking around the periphery of the playground. Sometimes he stands by one of the adults who is supervising recess or sits on the ground and picks at the grass. Other times he goes underneath the jungle gym and looks up through the cracks at the feet of children above him. The other second-graders are not unkind to Jeremy. But they do not seem to even notice that he is there. Aside from occasionally interacting with another student with a disability from his special education classroom, Jeremy does not talk to anyone at recess. Despite being on a playground with over one hundred other children, Jeremy is alone.

For most students, recess is a rich opportunity to grow friendships, build crucial social and communication skills, and develop their play. The American Academy of Pediatrics heralds recess as crucial for "optimizing a child's social emotional, physical, and cognitive development" (Murray et al., 2013, p. 186). But for students with significant disabilities like Jeremy, recess is often a missed opportunity.

What Is FLIP Recess?

FLIP recess stands for "focusing on learning, interaction, and play at recess." This approach combines two components to support students with significant disabilities who struggle to interact and play with their peers at recess. The first component, peer-mediated intervention, involves coaching peers to play with and support the student with a disability on the playground. An adult who is already supervising recess teaches peers practical strategies, grounded in pivotal response training (PRT; Pierce & Shreibman, 1995), that help to support the student's interactions and play. The same adult provides coaching at recess that enables the peers to successfully use the strategies. The second component, video modeling, aims to expand the student's repertoire of social and communication skills. Just before the student goes to recess, a teacher describes a social skill, shows the student a video that portrays use of the skill on the playground, and practices the skill with the student.

There are two reasons FLIP recess combines peer-mediated intervention with video modeling. First, new skills are best taught through a combination of focused instruction and opportunities to practice. This idea might be more intuitive when thinking about teaching an academic skill like early literacy. For example, providing a young child with lots of books is a great way to increase their opportunities to interact with text. However, the child is more likely to make progress if they also are receiving instruction on recognizing letters and their corresponding sounds. Once they have begun to make progress on basic phonics skills, there is a fundamental change in the way they are able to access the text in books. This same principle is true for promoting improved social skills at recess. Peer-mediated intervention alone is an evidence-based tool for increasing peer interactions (Hume et al., 2021). But students are much more likely to be successful in those interactions when they are also taught critical social skills, like how to respond to greetings, ask questions, give compliments, and keep a conversation going.

Second, it is simply more fun to play with someone who has better social skills. At their best, peer-mediated interventions are enjoyable and motivating for the peers who are providing support. Most peers would prefer to play with students who greet them warmly, take turns, and ask them about things they are interested in. In contrast, few peers are motivated to play with students who ignore them, refuse to share, and only want to talk about their own interests.

This is not to say that perfect social skills are a prerequisite for playing with peers. Indeed, peers often recognize and appreciate when a student is simply making an effort to expand their social skills.

What Types of Students Benefit From FLIP Recess?

FLIP recess is designed for students with significant disabilities who have limited or infrequent positive interactions with peers at recess. The following questions are designed to identify a student who would be a good fit for FLIP recess:

1. Does the student have a developmental disability (e.g., educational label of autism, intellectual disability, or multiple disabilities)?
2. Does the student have significant support needs that require curricular modifications and individualized intervention?
3. Does the student have limited or infrequent positive interactions with peers at recess?
4. Does the student have a history that is free of aggressive behavior or violence toward peers?

If the answer to all the above questions is yes, the student is likely a good candidate for FLIP recess. Note that FLIP recess was designed specifically for students with significant support needs. This means that the video modeling component focuses on very basic social skills. In addition, there is an assumption that peers already recognize that the student with a disability is different, and the student will not mind if a teacher discusses these differences with peers. In contrast, students on the autism spectrum who do not have significant support needs might be ready for more advanced social skills instruction, and they might object to a teacher discussing their differences with peers. Therefore, students on the autism spectrum who have less intensive support needs might not be a good fit for FLIP Recess. Other interventions, such as Remaking Recess (Shih et al., 2019) would likely be a better match for these students.

Who Can Implement FLIP Recess?

Implementing FLIP recess involves taking on two roles: providing video modeling instruction just before recess and coaching peers during recess. These roles can be performed by the same person or by two different people. Often, a classroom teacher or paraeducator is best positioned to provide video modeling instruction in the classroom, and an adult who was already responsible for supervising students on the playground is best positioned to coach peers at recess. In research studies, many different adults have successfully been peer coaches (Brock et al., 2018), including regular education teachers or paraeducators who were on recess duty as well as special education paraeducators who accompanied students with disabilities onto the playground. Because FLIP recess is feasible only when teachers partner with others, this chapter includes guidance for partnering with paraeducators.

A Step-By-Step Guide for Implementing FLIP Recess

This part of the chapter is a step-by-step guide to implementing FLIP recess. It includes forms and checklists that can be reproduced, guidance for partnering with paraeducators, a vignette that illustrates what FLIP recess looks like in action, and case studies that describe common obstacles and how to overcome them. Steps for implementation are split into the two components of FLIP recess: video modeling and peer-mediated intervention. Although video modeling is presented first and peer-mediated intervention is presented second in this section, in practice the two components occur simultaneously.

Video Modeling to Teach New Social Skills

Materials. Often, teachers can use technology that is already in their classroom or school to implement video modeling. All that is required is a means to record video clips and then play those video clips for the student. This might be easiest to do on a tablet computer so that the teacher can both record and play from the same device. However, there is no need to purchase a tablet specifically for this purpose. It is also possible to record on a phone or camcorder and then transfer the video files to a desktop or laptop computer for viewing.

Preparing and Planning. Start by identifying three to five social skills that the student has not yet mastered and that would help the student be more successful in their interactions and play with peers. Social skills that might be considered include appropriate greetings, on-topic questions, sharing materials, keeping the conversation going, and complimenting others. Next, the teacher should write a script for how the student could use each targeted social skill at recess. It is important to write the script in a way that could be reproduced by the student. For example, if the student uses sign language, the script should describe a child signing to communicate. Or if the student only speaks in two or three word phrases, the script should match this style of communication. Related to this point, the script should involve a social situation that the student is likely to encounter at recess. The teacher should plan where on the playground the social skill might be used, what the student will say or do, and what peers will say or do. Writing a detailed script will enable teachers to record high-quality videos more efficiently in the next step.

Recording and Reviewing. Next, teachers record a video for each social skill. Typically, it is most efficient to record peers who have already mastered the social skill, who take directions well, and who can memorize lines from a script. Teachers often record the videos with the same peers who will be helping to deliver the peer-mediated intervention, although recording the same peers is not required. Coach peers to project their voices to ensure that they can be heard on the recording. It is best to record videos at the playground locations where the student will most likely have opportunities to use the targeted skill. The idea is to make it as easy as possible for the student to envision how they could use the skill at recess.

Before showing the videos to the student, review the videos and rerecord if necessary. It is important to check that (a) it is easy to hear and understand what people are saying, (b) the social skill is clearly and correctly modeled; and (c) the video is free of any stimuli that might distract the student from focusing on the target skill.

FIGURE 5.1 Implementation Checklist for Video Modeling

1. **Briefly review the targeted social skill.**
   ☐ In a few sentences, define the social skill, give specific examples of what it might look like at recess, and describe why it is important.
   Example for Giving Compliments: A compliment is when you tell your friend that you like something about them or something they are doing. For example, you might tell your friend that you like their shoes,

that they are really good at soccer, or that you really enjoy spending time with them. It feels good to receive a compliment. Today we are going to watch a video about how you can give compliments to your friends at recess.

2. **Show the focal student the video model.**
   - ☐ Arrange the environment so that the video viewing equipment is in front of the student with a significant disability and so that they are focused on it.
   - ☐ If the student is unable to focus, try using a reward system, such as one they use while completing work in class. You can try to take the student to a less distracting environment. If the student does well with mindfulness activities, you could try one of those here as well.

3. **Role-play the skill with the focal student.**
   - ☐ Tell the student that you will take turns practicing the skill and that you will go first.
   - ☐ Model how to use the social skill in the same way it was demonstrated in the video.
   - ☐ Prompt the student with a significant disability to practice the skill in the same way it was demonstrated in the video. Use the video script if needed.
   - ☐ Praise the student for correct performance.
   - ☐ If needed, help the student correct their mistakes and practice again.

4. **Set a goal with the focal student for how they will use the social skill at recess.**
   - ☐ Work with the student to set a goal for how they could use the skill at recess.

      Examples of goals: greet three friends at recess, ask a friend two on-topic questions, offer a friend a turn with your chalk, give a friend at least two compliments

Lesson Delivery. For a checklist of steps for implementing a video modeling lesson, see Figure 5.1. First, the teacher briefly introduces the social skill by defining, providing examples, and describing why it is important. For example, if teaching how to give compliments, a teacher might say: "A compliment is when you tell your friend that you like something about them or something they are doing. For example, you might tell your friend that you like their shoes, that they are really good at soccer, or that you really enjoy spending time with them. It feels good to get a compliment. Today we are going to watch a video about how you can give compliments to your friends at recess." Second, the teacher shows the target student the video model. It is important to arrange the environment so that the video is directly in front of the student and there are minimal distractions. If the student struggles to focus on the video, it may be helpful to review expectations before starting the video or tie watching the video to earning a reward. Third, the teacher uses role play to help the student practice the skill. The teacher starts by replicating the social skill in the same way that was demonstrated in the video and then prompts the student to practice the skill in the same way. The teacher praises the student for what they did well and, if necessary, helps the student correct their mistakes and practice again.

Fourth, the teacher helps the student set a goal for how they will use the social skill at recess. For example, if targeting greetings, the student might set the goal: "Greet three friends at recess." Or if targeting compliments, the student might set a goal to give a friend two compliments. Goals should be objective, attainable, and easily understood by the student.

Peer-Mediated Intervention: New Opportunities for Social Interaction

The second component, peer-mediated intervention, involves selecting and recruiting peer buddies, providing initial peer training, and offering ongoing coaching and support on the playground.

Selecting and Recruiting Peer Buddies. It is best for teachers to recruit three to five students who will be peer buddies for the student. At least three are needed to establish a network where peers are supporting one another and to increase the likelihood that at least one peer buddy will be present at recess. In addition, it is not unusual for children to play with different groups of friends at recess. Having three peer buddies provides flexibility for peers to take turns naturally shifting between playing with the student and with other friends. Limiting formal training and coaching to five peer buddies does not limit the number of peers that the student can play with. On the contrary, training a small group of peer buddies is just a manageable starting point for expanding the number of peers with which the student interacts and plays.

When selecting peer buddies, consider children who (a) have good attendance, (b) have strong social and play skills, and (c) respond well to suggestions from adults. In addition, peers who have shown interest in or have interacted positively with the student are often good choices. While there might be a natural inclination to recruit the highest performing or best-behaved peers, neither is a requirement for being an effective peer buddy.

Teachers may find it helpful to have conversations with students with disabilities and their families about which peers they most prefer. Part of these conversations should focus on the degree to which students would prefer to include peers who share their own gender, race, culture, or primary language in their playgroup. For example, a third-grade Latina whose family speaks Spanish at home might enjoy playing with another girl who also speaks Spanish. Or a Black first-grade boy might prefer for his peer buddies to include another Black boy. In sum, it is important to honor the preferences of the student and their family and not make assumptions about their preferences without asking them. In research studies, students have responded well to diverse groups of peer buddies that include both peers who do and who do not share their race, culture, primary language, or gender (Amadi et al., 2022). After identifying potential peer buddies, talk with peers to confirm their interest and then communicate with their families. A sample permission for families of potential peer buddies is included in Figure 5.2.

FIGURE 5.2 Sample Permission Form for Families of Peer Buddies

Dear Parents and Families,
One of your child's teachers has recommended your child to be a peer buddy for *FLIP recess*, an intervention designed to support students with disabilities at recess. Your child was recommended because they have great social skills and show kindness and patience with others.

If it is okay with you, we would like to teach your child some simple strategies to interact and play at recess with a child who has a disability. Your child would be one of several children who would be taught to use these strategies. One of the adults who is supervising recess would monitor what is happening, regularly check in with your child, and provide support to make sure that recess continues to be a fun time for everyone involved.

Please send this form to your child's teacher to let us know if it is okay with you for your child to participate in FLIP recess as a peer buddy.

Check one:

_____ **Yes**, I give permission for my child to be a peer buddy at recess.

_____ **No**, I do not give permission for my child to be a peer buddy at recess.

Your Signature _____ Date _____

Initial Training for Peer Buddies. Once peers are selected, the coach will need to orient them to their new roles during an initial training session. This usually takes about half an hour and should be done in a place that is away from other students. Often it is convenient to meet with peers over lunch in an empty classroom. Other options include before school, after school, or during the school day at a time negotiated with the peers' teachers.

Initial training involves eight steps that are detailed below and summarized in the initial meeting implementation checklist in Figure 5.3. First, if they do not already know each other well, the coach introduces themself and has peers introduce themselves to one another. Second, the coach describes the purpose of being a peer buddy. For example, they might describe how some students struggle to make new friends and play with other kids at recess and that peer buddies can help make this easier for them. Coaches can also share that being a peer buddy should be fun. Other kids who have been peer buddies have talked about learning to play in new ways, learning new ways to communicate, and getting to make new friends with both the target student and the other peer buddies (Brock et al., 2018).

FIGURE 5.3 Implementation Checklist for Initial Peer Training

☐ **Introduce peers to each other** if they do not already know each other well.

☐ **Explain the purpose of being a peer buddy.** Explain that it is hard for the student to make new friends and play with other kids at recess and that peer buddies can help the student to interact and play with other kids in new ways.

☐ **Share background information about the student** from the background sheet that will be useful to the peer buddies (Figure 5.4).

- ☐ **Introduce FLIP recess strategies** from the strategy sheet in Figure 5.5. Read each strategy from the strategy sheet, model how to use it, invite peers to ask questions, and then guide the peers to practice through role play. Provide praise and support as appropriate.
- ☐ **Explain what peer buddy roles will look like.** Emphasize that being a peer buddy should be fun and that you will be there to support them
- ☐ **Encourage peers to talk about the student in the same way they would want a friend to talk about them.** It is fine for peer buddies to talk with others about what they are doing in a positive way, but it is not okay to talk about the student in a way that is negative or might embarrass the student.
- ☐ **Talk with peers about what they are most excited about and most nervous about.** Respond to each student and provide support and assurance as needed.
- ☐ **Tell peers when they will start being a peer buddy**—often the same day or the following day. Tell them that before recess, you will help each of them set a goal about how they will play with the student.

Third, the coach shares background information about the student that will be useful to the peer buddies. See Figures 5.7 and 5.4 for a blank and completed sample form for recording and sharing background information. This includes describing what the student is currently doing at recess, including missed opportunities for interaction and play. For example, a student might be walking on the periphery of the playground without ever talking or playing with anyone else. It also includes a list of play activities that the student might enjoy at recess. Examples could include any appropriate activity, such as playing tag, pretend play, drawing with chalk, hanging on bars, swinging, or playing basketball. Next, the coach describes how the student communicates and strategies for communicating effectively with the student. For example, a coach might explain that a student communicates in short spoken phrases and gestures and then provide examples of some of the gestures that they use. For students who use alternative and augmentative communication (AAC), it is important to help peers get comfortable with how to interact with the student. This might include bringing a speech-generating device to the peer training and demonstrating how the student uses it to communicate. It can be helpful to draw attention to areas of communication that are not yet within the student's repertoire so that peers do not get frustrated or confused by the student. For example, some peers might wonder why a student never asks *them* what *they* want to play until they understand that the student has a difficult time formulating questions. The background sheet should also include other information that could help peers successfully interact with the student. For example, if a student dislikes being touched unexpectedly, a coach might encourage peers to discuss with the student how they might be touched in advance of a game (e.g., being tapped on the back or forearm during tag). Or if a student's automatic reaction to any yes/no question is always "no," peers might be coached to say, "I would love it if you would come swing with me" instead of "Do you want to come swing with me?"

FIGURE 5.4 Example of a Completed Background Sheet

Right now ____Chloe____ is . . .

Describe what the focus student is doing at recess right now:

> At recess, Chloe swings on the swings by herself and does not talk to any other students. She spends her recess time alone unless another student swings next to her. When other students talk to Chloe, she makes noises and hand gestures. Chloe looks and smiles at other peers while swinging on the swings.

I think that with your help, ____Chloe____ might really enjoy . . .

List of play activities the focus student might enjoy at outdoor recess:

1. Jumping rope
2. Sliding
3. Playing tag
4. Swinging

____Chloe____ communicates . . .

Describe how the student communicates:

> Chloe uses simple sounds, pictures, and gestures to communicate. At recess, she brings a ring of pictures and words that she will point at to communicate. These are words like "Hi," "Yes," "All done," and her favorite activities. She will point at things to make choices or tell you what she needs. Chloe smiles and laughs at peers when she is having fun. Chloe answers yes/no questions by shaking her head yes or no.

This means that when you talk with _____Chloe_____ you will want to . . .

Describe how peers should communicate with student:

> *Use simple words with Chloe. Show her pictures or objects of things to let her make choices. You can use her pictures on her picture ring or physical objects on the playground. Watch what Chloe plays with to see what she likes. Ask Chloe yes/no questions and she will answer by shaking her head yes or no.*

There are also some other things about _____Chloe_____ that might be helpful to know.

List other information that peers might need to know to successfully interact with student:

> *Sometimes Chloe will look like she is staring at nothing. This can mean she is having a seizure. This means something is happening in her brain that makes her see and feel things differently for a little bit, so it may seem like she does not know you are there. Usually this lasts just for a few seconds, and then she is back to her regular self. It seems to make her feel better after a seizure if someone is close to her and talking softly to her. If you can count to 10 and Chloe still does not seem back to her regular self, come tell me.*

Note: Adapted with permission from Brock (2022).

Fourth, the coach shares the strategies from the strategy sheet in Figure 5.5. These include getting your buddy to look at you, asking your buddy to play something with you, showing and talking about how to play, praising your buddy, and taking turns. For each strategy, the coach first reads the strategy from the strategy sheet, models how to use it, invites and answers questions from peers, and then sets up a role play situation for the peers to practice the strategy. This involves the coach pretending they are the student and each peer having an opportunity to practice the strategy. The coach praises what the peers do well and provides supportive feedback when needed. Fifth, the coach shares that they will be present at recess and support peers as they take on their new roles as peer buddies. The coach emphasizes that being a peer buddy should be fun. So if peers are not having fun, they need to let the coach know so the coach can try to help fix it. Sixth, the coach encourages peers to talk about the student in the same way they would want a friend to talk about them. The coach explains that it is fine to share about what they are doing in a positive way. For example, it would be fine to tell another friend that they are helping the student to learn new ways to play or talk to a friend about the best ways to communicate with the student. On the other hand, peers should avoid emphasizing things that the student struggles with or sharing information that might embarrass the student. Seventh, the coach asks peer buddies what they are most excited about and most nervous about. The coach responds to each peer and provides support and assurance as needed. Finally, the coach talks to the peers about when they will begin providing support at recess—often the same day or the following day. The coach shares that before recess, they will meet with each peer to have them set a goal about how they will play with the student. The coach will write down the goal and check in with each peer at the end of recess to see if they met their goal.

Ongoing Coaching to Support Peer Buddies. Initial training is important to help peer buddies get off to a good start but is insufficient without ongoing coaching on the playground. Coaching is the key to supporting peers to apply the strategies they learned, to navigate new or unexpected situations, and to maintain interactions and play that are mutually enjoyed by both the student and the peer buddies. FLIP recess coaching strategies were designed to be feasible for adults who are responsible for supervising all students at recess. Typically, the coach cannot devote their undivided attention to coaching peers for the entire recess period, so the following strategies involve providing sporadic and targeted support. Coaching steps are detailed below and summarized in the Peer Buddy Coaching Implementation Checklist in Figure 5.6.

FIGURE 5.6 Implementation Checklist for Coaching Peer Buddies at Recess

- [ ] **Help peer buddies set goals at the beginning of recess.** Each day at recess, ask each peer buddy to set their own goal about how they will try to play or interact with their buddy. This can be simple, like "I am going to ask Eddie to play basketball with me" or "I am going to try to show Veronica how to jump rope." If more than one peer buddy wants to work on the same goal together, that's fine. Record their goals on your clipboard using a dry erase marker.

- [ ] **Praise peer buddies when they are doing well**. Find opportunities to let peers know they are doing well and that you are proud of them. You could

FIGURE 5.5 Strategy Sheet for Coaching Peers to Implement
FLIP Recess Strategies

Get your buddy to look at you.

If you want to talk to your buddy and your buddy isn't looking at you, get their attention:

1. Say your buddy's name.
2. Look at your buddy's eyes.
3. If your buddy still isn't looking at you, ask them to look at you.

Be patient. Sometimes it might take a little while to get your buddy's attention. Your buddy might look at your face but not your eyes.

Ask your buddy to play something with you.

- If your buddy isn't playing with anyone, ask them if they want to play something with you.

- Try to think of something to play that you think your buddy will like.
- Sometimes it helps to offer more than one idea to play, and you can let your buddy choose.

Show and talk about how to play.
- If your buddy isn't sure how to play something, show them how to do it.
- Talk about what you are doing as you show them.

Praise your buddy.
- Tell your buddy they are doing a good job when they try something.
- You can also give your buddy a high five, fist bump, or pat on the back.

If you can't play at the same time, take turns with your buddy.
- When it's time to change turns, explain to your buddy what is happening.

Note: Reproduced with permission from Brock (2022).

tell them that they are doing a great job or that you are proud of them, but sometimes it might be easier to give a quick high five or a thumbs up across the playground.

☐ **Provide support when peer buddies are struggling.** Keep an eye on how things are going. If you see that any of the peer buddies or the student with a significant disability is frustrated or not having a good time or that things could be going better, help the peer buddies to take a different approach. Remind them of the strategies on your clipboard.

☐ **Even if things are going well, check in to see if peer buddies have questions or need help.** At least once at recess, walk over and ask the peer buddies how things are going and offer your help.

☐ **Check in at the end of recess to see if peer buddies met their goals.** At the end of recess, show peer buddies their goals on the clipboard and ask them if they met their goals. If they did, be sure to praise them. If they did not, ask them if there is anything that you can do to help meet them next time.

Note: Adapted with permission from Brock (2022).

First, coaches should talk with peers at the beginning of recess, or just before recess, to help them set goals. Depending on the availability of the coach and the peers, this might happen in the lunchroom, while students are lined up to go to outside, or at the beginning of recess. Goals should describe ways that the peers hope to interact or play with the student. Sometimes goals might align with a specific FLIP recess strategy. For example, a peer might say, "I am going to help Trevor understand the rules of tag by talking through who is 'it' and how I am trying to run away so they can't touch me." Other times, goals might just relate to general ways that a peer aims to engage the student. Once peers get to know the student, they may have specific examples of ways the student might enjoy interacting. For example, a peer might set a goal to "Make chalk drawings with Jamaal," "Pretend to be Spiderman characters with Sophie," or "Talk with Sara about football." Either of these approaches to goals is fine— the important thing is for peers to visualize a way that they can interact or play with the student. The coach should record the peer buddy goals on a dry erase clipboard or a piece of paper so that they can be revisited after recess.

Next, the coach intermittently observes the peer buddies and the student and assesses if and what type of support might be needed. There will be times when the peer buddies are unsure what to do, when one or more peer buddies or the student seems frustrated, when there are missed opportunities, or when peers are unsure how to engage with the student. In these situations, the coach needs to step in to offer suggestions or to model alternative ways to interact and play. Especially at first, there are often situations in which the coach may need to step in to kickstart a conversation or game as the peer buddies and student are just getting to know one another. It is equally important to let peers know when they are doing a great job. In situations when the peers and student are actively playing, the best way to do this might be a thumbs up, which communicates approval without interrupting their play. As the peer buddies and student become more comfortable with one another, the coach's role often shifts to troubleshooting and being a resource for the peers. Occasionally checking in with peers continues to be important, even if from a distance it appears that things are going well.

At the end of recess, coaches should talk with peers to revisit their goals. Natural times for this might be just before the recess whistle, as students are lining up to go back inside, or as peers are walking back to their classroom. If one of the peers did not meet their goal, they and the coach can discuss why things did not work out and what they might do differently next time. This is also an opportunity to praise peers for how they supported the student and used the FLIP recess strategies.

Troubleshooting

Often the trickiest part of coaching is handling situations at recess when peers are frustrated or unsure what to do. The following case studies illustrate examples of challenges and how a peer buddy coach can resolve them.

CASE STUDY 1: Eddie doesn't know how to play tag.

PROBLEM. Ms. Waters supervises second-grade recess and volunteers to coach peer buddies to support Eddie—a student on the autism spectrum who communicates mostly through gestures and a tablet that is loaded with Proloquo2Go. At first, things seem to get off to a great start with Eddie and his peer buddies. One buddy asks Eddie if he wants to play tag, and he says yes. But once they start playing tag, Eddie only seems to understand that he should try to run away, and he continues to run away from his peer buddies even when he is supposed to be "it." One of the peer buddies approaches Ms. Waters and says, "It really isn't fun to play with Eddie anymore. He only wants to play tag but he doesn't understand how to play."

SOLUTION. Ms. Waters talks to the peers to help problem solve. First, she checks if it would be better to keep playing tag or to switch to a different game. She asks the peers if they are tired of playing tag and want to play something different. They say that the enjoy playing tag but just do not see how they can play tag with Eddie because he does not follow the rules. Ms. Waters gives the peers some suggestions. She explains that from what she can see, Eddie loves being chased and just doesn't understand how and when to switch from being chased to being "it." She suggests that maybe they and Eddie will have more fun if they play in a way that they don't ever expect him to be "it." Maybe instead, whoever is "it" can chase Eddie for part of their turn, and then chase and tag a different friend to be "it." At the same time, they can talk about their play to Eddie and maybe he will start to catch on to the rules of tag. So, if they get tagged and are close to Eddie, they can tell him "I just got tagged, so now it is my turn to be 'it.' I am going to chase other people and try to tag them."

OUTCOME. The peers try Ms. Waters's suggestions. Their frustration subsides once they understand that it is okay for Eddie to participate just by running away and never being "it." They do narrate the rules of tag to Eddie as they play, but Eddie takes little notice and continues to play in the same way by running away. Eddie seems to be having a great time and smiles and laughs every time he is chased. Ms. Waters praises the peer buddies for including Eddie in a way that everyone has fun.

CASE STUDY 2: Cadence says no to everything.

PROBLEM. Mr. Olsen supervises fourth and fifth grade recess and volunteers to coach peer buddies to support Cadence—a fourth-grader with Down syndrome who talks in single words or short phrases. Before Mr. Olsen started working with the peer buddies, Cadence would sit by herself on a bench and sing to herself. After Mr. Olsen trains the peer buddies, they are excited to play with Cadence, but Cadence does not seem to be excited to play with them. They ask her to play soccer, and she says, "No way." They invite her to play a half dozen other activities but continue to get the same response. They do not ask Mr. Olsen for help, but he can see that they are exasperated.

SOLUTION. Mr. Olsen pulls the peers aside to talk. He praises them for trying so hard to invite Cadence to play, says he is sorry that Cadence has given them such a negative response, and suggests they brainstorm together what they can do. They come up with three different ideas. First, instead of asking Cadence yes/no questions, they will give Cadence options. They try to come up with options that she might want to choose. They revisit the ideas that they wrote down during the peer buddy training. Second, Mr. Olsen suggests that maybe sometimes they could just have a conversation with Cadence on the bench about things that they have in common. He reminds them that she likes to listen to JoJo Siwa and watch Bluey. He reminds them that she has a dog named Lucky and that she likes to bowl with her Special Olympics team. Third, Mr. Olsen suggests that even if Cadence says no to everything, they could play something that she might like nearby and see if she decides to join on her own. Mr. Olsen says that once they start playing, he can encourage her to join.

OUTCOME. At first, Cadence still says "no way" even when she is offered options that include activities that she enjoys. But she loves when the peers talk with her, and if they play something nearby that she enjoys—like drawing with chalk or jumping rope—she often joins with a little encouragement from Mr. Olsen. Over time, she begins to start playing with peers as soon as they offer play options, but on other days, they still get a "no way" and it takes coaxing from Mr. Olsen to get her up from the bench. Mr. Olsen praises the peers and tells them how proud he is of them and how excited he is that they are finding ways to play with Cadence. He tells them that he is especially proud of how they continue trying even though Cadence does not always make it easy for them. He says that it is clear to him that once she actually starts playing or talking with them that she is having a great time.

CASE STUDY 3: Amari just wants to do the same thing every day, and it is getting boring.

PROBLEM. At first, Ms. Harrison is thrilled with how the peer buddies are engaging with Amari. They have settled into a routine of talking together and drawing with chalk on the blacktop. But after about a week, one of the peers tells Ms. Harrison that she wants to stop being Amari's peer buddy. When asked why, the peer shares that she wants to run around and play tag or soccer and that Amari only wants to sit and draw every day and that it is getting boring.

SOLUTION. Ms. Harrison talks with all the peer buddies together and asks if they are feeling the same way. It turns out that the other two peers are still having a great time and say that often they would draw with chalk even if they were not playing with Amari. Ms. Harrison tells the first peer that the goal of being a peer buddy is for everyone to have fun and that she shouldn't feel like she needs to keep drawing with chalk if she would prefer to play tag or soccer. She encourages her to go play other games but to know that she is always welcome to stop by to talk or draw with Amari and the other peer buddies.

OUTCOME. The peer buddy plays soccer most days at recess but stops and talks with Amari and the other peer buddies a couple times each week. Ms. Harrison tells her that this is just fine. Like with any friend, it is okay not to want to play the same thing with them every day.

Partnering with Paraeducators

In most situations, it is not feasible for one teacher to implement FLIP recess alone. Often, the key to success is teaming with paraeducators who are already supporting the student or already are supervising recess. There are proven training and supervision strategies that set paraeducators up to be successful (Brock & Anderson, 2021). These include defining roles, explaining how the intervention will benefit the student, walking through a checklist of steps, modeling the steps, and observing and providing feedback. This section describes how to apply each of these strategies to FLIP recess.

Define Roles

It is the teacher's responsibility to plan and design the intervention. This means the teacher is responsible for identifying students who would benefit from the intervention, identifying peers who will provide support, writing the background information that will be shared with peers, selecting social skills that will be targeted, and writing scripts for how the social skills will be portrayed in video models. In their leadership role, it is appropriate for teachers to solicit input from the paraeducators, especially in situations where the paraeducators might be more familiar with peers or with the student's behavior at recess. Appropriate roles for paraeducators include implementing the initial peer training, coaching peers on the playground, recording video models, and implementing video models with the student. Teachers should be explicit about which of these roles they are asking paraeducators to do.

Talk About the Benefits for the Student

Describe how recruiting, training, and coaching peers has the potential to substantially increase opportunities for students with disabilities to interact, play, and build friendships with peers. Next, highlight how video modeling has the potential to build and expand social skills by showing students exactly how to use these skills at recess. Teachers can share that FLIP recess is not a new or untested approach, but a strategy that has worked well for students with disabilities in research studies.

Walk Through the Checklist

Provide paraeducators with one or more checklists that match their new responsibilities. For example, Figure 5.3 describes steps for conducting an initial peer training, Figure 5.5 describes how to coach peers at recess, and Figure 5.1 describes how to implement a video modeling lesson. Walk through each step of the checklist while providing an explanation and examples of what each step entails. Teachers may find it helpful to simultaneously refer to the checklist and the main text of this chapter that provide explanation and examples.

Model the Steps

Paraeducators are most likely to implement the steps as designed after observing a teacher do it first. With the paraeducator observing, implement an initial training, coach peers at recess, and deliver a video modeling lesson. Paraeducators can be active observers by following along with an implementation checklist from Figures 5.1, 5.3, or 5.6 as they observe.

Observe and Provide Feedback

Observe the paraeducator when they implement their first initial peer training, when they provide coaching for the first time at recess, when they implement their first video modeling lesson, and then intermittently over time. Use the implementation checklist as a guide for supporting the paraeducator during the initial peer training. For the initial peer training and video modeling, the implementation checklist provides a sequential list of straightforward steps. If the paraeducator misses one of the steps, the teacher can step in to help make sure that it gets covered. If the problem was just forgetting to do the step, the teacher might just point to the step to remind the paraeducator. If the paraeducator is unsure what to do, the teacher might remodel implementation of that step.

Helping a paraeducator to provide coaching at recess can be more challenging. Although there are implementation steps detailed in Figure 5.5, there are also elements of judgement and improvisation about when and how to provide support based on individual students and situations. For example, paraeducators must be able to identify when things are going well and they should step back and when there are challenges and they need to step in. In addition, paraeducators will need to make judgments about how much structure is required when providing support. Supporting paraeducators with these skills is not as simple as pointing out a missed step on a checklist and often will require more dialogue. One approach is for teachers to talk out loud about what they are observing and why and how they are deciding to intervene based on what they see. Sharing their decision-making process out loud in real-time can help the paraeducator understand how to make similar decisions in the future. It may also be helpful to talk through the case studies in this chapter that illustrate how to troubleshoot when peers are frustrated or unsure what to do.

FLIP Recess in Action

The following vignette, a composite of real experiences, illustrates what FLIP recess looks like in action. You'll recall Jeremy, the second-grader described at the beginning of this chapter, who often played alone on the playground. Below you'll read how Jeremy's teacher used FLIP recess to transform recess into a meaningful opportunity for socialization and peer play.

Jeremy's teacher, Ms. Abrams, reads about FLIP recess—an intervention that is designed to increase interactions, play, and social skills on the playground. Her mind goes straight to Jeremy. As she reads, she gets excited about the idea of transforming recess into a meaningful opportunity for Jeremy to build social skills and relationships with peers. Ms. Abrams starts thinking about logistics. Her only break from students during the day is during their lunch and recess, and she does not want to give that up. She knows that she will need to team up with other staff to pull this off.

First, Ms. Abrams meets with her assistant principal to describe FLIP recess and ask for support with teaming up with other staff. Together, Ms. Abrams and the assistant principal talk with Mr. Jones, one of the paraeducators who supervises the recess that Jeremy attends. When Mr. Jones is not supervising recess, he is working in a regular education second-grade classroom. Mr. Jones is excited about the idea of supporting Jeremy. After spending many recess periods with Jeremy standing beside him or watching Jeremy pick grass, he would love to contribute to a positive change. At the same time, Mr. Jones shares that he is not sure if he is the right person for the job—he does not have any experience in special education and does not typically work directly with Ms. Abrams. Ms. Abrams assures Mr. Jones that he is exactly the right person for the job—he knows Jeremy well, has a great relationship with the second-grade students, and is already out on the playground every day. Ms. Abrams explains that his role will be coaching four peers to use five simple strategies to interact and play with Jeremy at recess. She walks him through the steps for training and coaching peers at recess.

Next, Ms. Abrams starts a FLIP recess plan by filling out a background information sheet. She jots down a description of Jeremy's interests at recess and how he communicates. She also identifies social skills that could help Jeremy be more successful at recess. She identifies four skills—initiating a greeting, giving compliments, sharing materials with others, and asking on-topic questions. She writes short scripts for how Jeremey could use each of these skills at recess. Then, Ms. Abrams chats with Mr. Jones and several of the second-grade regular-education teachers about peers who have good social skills, who respond well to feedback from adults, and who would be the most likely to enjoy playing with Jeremy. She also asks Jeremy if there are any friends he would enjoy playing with. In addition, she calls Jeremy's family to tell them about FLIP recess and ask for their input for selecting peers. After identifying four peers, Ms. Abrams sends permission forms home to their families.

Once the forms are returned, Ms. Abrams works with the peers to create video models for the skills she identified. For the first video, she has one of the peers stand under the playground equipment where Jeremy usually stands. Another peer comes up and greets him, and the peer playing Jeremy looks up to make eye contact, smiles, and says "hi" back. They shoot each of the four videos and check each one to make sure that the audio is understandable and the social skill is clearly demonstrated.

Ms. Abrams meets with both of her classroom paraeducators before school to walk them through how to use video modeling with Jeremy. First, she explains that video modeling is part of a larger effort to help Jeremy improve his social interactions and relationships at recess. She explains that video modeling is a proven strategy, in part because showing a child with a disability exactly what a skill looks like can be more effective than just talking about it. She provides a checklist of the key steps of how to implement a video modeling lesson and talks them through each step. Ms. Abrams knows she does not have the staff to have both paraeducators observe her modeling the steps with Jeremy at the same time, so she has one paraeducator observe her the first day and the other observe her the next day. Then she has the paraeducators each give it a try. She observes each of them and follows *along with the checklist. One paraeducator forgets to guide the student to set goals, so she gently prompts them by pointing to that step on the checklist. Afterward she praises them for doing so well on their first attempt. The paraeducators take over responsibility for implementing the video models, but Ms. Abrams checks in with them regularly to make sure things are going well, and she observes part of a lesson at least once a week.*

As she works to get the video modeling up and running with her classroom paraeducators, Ms. Abrams also sets up an initial peer training with Mr. Jones and the four peers. Ms. Abrams explains to Mr. Jones that she will model how to do the peer training this time, and then he will be ready to lead peer trainings for other students in the future. Ms. Abrams makes sure that both she and Mr. Jones have the initial peer training checklist in front of them as she goes through each step. The peers are very excited to get started.

During the first recess after the meeting, Ms. Abrams goes out to model how to coach peers while Mr. Jones follows along on the checklist. She meets with the peers to discuss goals for recess. Next, she steps in to make sure the peers and Jeremy get off to a good start. Once they are happily engaged in a game of tag, Ms. Abrams backs off and talks with Mr. Jones. She explains that he won't need to stay close to the peers during the whole recess—the goal is to get things off to a good start, jump in when needed, and wrap up at the end. After recess she shows Mr. Jones how to check with each peer and discuss whether they met their goals. The next day Mr. Jones starts to provide coaching to the peers. He is a natural—Ms. Abrams compliments him on a job well done and explains that she will come observe that last few minutes of recess about once a week to see how things are going. She encourages Mr. Jones to reach out if he experiences any challenges.

As the weeks go by, Mr. Jones flourishes in his role as a peer buddy coach. He has a knack for knowing when to step in to smooth out disagreements and misunderstandings and how to back off when Jeremy and his new friends are playing well together and having a good time. Jeremy has not completely mastered the social skills from the video models, but he is making progress. Jeremy's peers get excited when he comes up and greets them for the first time—they had grown accustomed to always having to be the ones to initiate with him. At first some of his compliments are a little awkward—he compliments all four of them on their shoes—but they love that he is trying to say kind things to them. Sometimes the new friends still play tag, but other times they draw with chalk or play basketball. Not every peer plays with Jeremy for the whole recess each day. They begin to naturally shift their time between playing with Jeremy and playing with other friends.

Ms. Abrams is thrilled with how well things are going. When she touches base with both Mr. Jones and her classroom paraeducators, she makes sure to tell them how pleased she is with Jeremy's growth and everything they are doing to support him. She and Mr. Jones begin to discuss how to put FLIP recess in place for other students with significant disabilities.

Conclusion

With FLIP recess, teachers can transform recess into a rich opportunity for developing social skills and friendships. This approach combines a peer-mediated intervention that increases peer interaction with video modeling that promotes social skills. These components work together by creating new opportunities for peer interaction and by supporting students to be successful in those interactions. Like many interventions for students with significant disabilities, FLIP recess is only feasible when teachers effectively partner with paraeducators. Together, teachers and paraeducators can support all students to experience the full benefits of recess.

FIGURE 5.7 Blank Background Sheet

Right now _____ is . . .

Describe what the focus student is doing at recess right now:

I think that with your help, _____ might really enjoy . . .

List of play activities the focus student might enjoy at outdoor recess:

    1.

    2.

    3.

    4.

_____ communicates . . .

Describe how the student communicates:

This means that when you talk with _____ you will want to . . .

Describe how peers should communicate with student:

There are also some other things about _____ that might be helpful to know.

List other information that peers might need to know to successfully interact with student:

Note: Adapted with permission from Brock (2022).

6

Peer Tutoring: Providing Targeted Instruction

Jordan is a third-grader with intellectual disability who splits his day between special and regular education classrooms. One of the blocks of time that Jordan spends in the regular education class is for literacy. Jordan is still a beginning reader and is not ready to read text at a third-grade level. During independent reading time, Jordan sits with a peer who reads the book aloud. Jordan loves when his peers read to him. He also enjoys being able to participate in discussions of the text during reading groups. These activities allow Jordan to access grade-level text, but they do little to help him with early reading skills.

To teach Jordan early literacy skills, Jordan's special education teacher, Ms. Donovan, provides targeted instruction in the special education classroom. This includes basic instruction on phonics and sight words as well as beginning level readers that apply these skills in the text. At his individualized education program (IEP) meeting, Jordan's parents advocate for him to spend more time in the general education classroom. Ms. Donovan explains that the main reason that he spends time in the special education classroom is because some of his goals are not addressed in the instruction that is happening in the regular education classroom. For example, Jordan needs basic phonics and sight word instruction that is not part of the third-grade curriculum. Jordan's

*parents agree that he needs focused instruction on early literacy skills
but wish there were a way to address more of Jordan's instructional
needs in the regular education classroom.*

When students with significant disabilities are behind grade level on academic skills, teachers sometimes presume that they will need substantial instruction outside of the regular education classroom to meet their needs. While it is true that students with significant disabilities often require academic instruction beyond what is naturally provided in the regular education classroom, it is a mistake to presume that this instruction must occur in a separate classroom. Indeed, there are proven approaches for providing supplemental instruction within the regular education classroom. One of these approaches, peer tutoring, involves a peer providing short doses of supplemental academic instruction in the regular education classroom (Jameson et al., 2008). Not only can this approach improve academic outcomes for students with significant disabilities (Hudson et al., 2014), but peers can also benefit. Specifically, peers may themselves develop a deeper understanding of academic content, learn how to better monitor their own learning, and improve their ability to follow written directions (Travers & Carter, 2022).

What Is Peer Tutoring?

Peer tutoring involves training and supervising peers to deliver focused academic instruction to students with significant disabilities in regular education classrooms. This approach is distinct from peer support arrangements, which involve general academic and social support over a long period of time. In peer tutoring, peers are focused solely on providing brief academic instruction related to specific goals (Jameson et al., 2008). The emphasis is not on building social relationships, but the student and peers often enjoy working together. Peer tutoring is flexible and can be applied to a range of academic outcomes. If a teacher has introduced an academic skill and the student would benefit from short and frequent doses of practice, that skill is likely a good candidate for peer tutoring. Examples of skills one might want to target include defining science vocabulary words, answering basic math facts, identifying sight words, answering reading comprehension questions, identifying letters and their sounds, and applying phonics knowledge to read decodable words (Hudson et al., 2014, Jimenez et al., 2012; Ley Davis et al., 2022).

What Types of Students Benefit From Peer Tutoring?

Peer tutoring is designed for students with significant disabilities who would benefit from short and frequent opportunities to practice academic skills beyond what is already provided in the regular education classroom. The following questions are designed to identify a student who would be a good fit for peer tutoring:

1. Does the student have a developmental disability (e.g., educational label of autism, intellectual disability, or multiple disabilities)?
2. Would the student benefit from short and frequent opportunities to practice one or more academic skills beyond what is already provided in the regular education classroom?
3. Are their adequate behavioral supports in place for the student to work well with a peer for short periods of time?

If the answer to all the above questions is yes, a student is likely a good candidate for peer tutoring.

Who Can Implement Peer Tutoring?

Most often, a general education teacher and special education teacher will need to work together to design peer tutoring, and peers will receive training and coaching from either a teacher or a paraeducator. The special education teacher is best positioned to select academic targets and design an instructional strategy for peers to use. The general education teacher is best positioned to propose the logistics for how peer tutoring will be integrated into the classroom schedule. Often, a paraeducator is best positioned to train and coach peers to be successful. However, paraeducators will need to be fluent in the teacher-designed instructional approach before they are ready to train peers.

A Step-By-Step Guide for Implementing Peer Tutoring

This part of the chapter is a step-by-step guide to implementing peer tutoring. It includes forms and checklists that can be reproduced, guidance for partnering with paraeducators, a vignette that illustrates what peer tutoring looks like in action, and case studies that describe common obstacles and how to overcome them.

Initial Planning

Initial planning involves identifying an instructional target, selecting an approach, designing data collection, writing clear steps for peers, and working out logistics. A planning sheet for working through these steps is provided at the end of the chapter in Figure 6.5, a sample of a completed sheet is provided in Table 6.1, and each of the steps is described in detail below, in Figure 6.1.

FIGURE 6.1 Example Initial Planning Sheet for Peer Tutoring

1. Identify an Academic Target

What academic skill will be the focus on peer tutoring? This should be one or more academic skills for which the student would benefit from short and frequent opportunities to practice, beyond what is already provided in the regular education classroom.

Basic math facts

2. Identify an Instructional Approach and Design Steps for Peers

What instructional approach will peers use to target the skill? Consider using proven approaches, such as time delay or least-to-most prompting. Record the name of your approach below.

Time delay

3. Design a Data Collection System

Describe how you plan to collect data on student progress. Will peers, teachers, or the student be responsible for recording correct responses?

On the last time through the deck of flash cards, the peer will put facts that the student knew independently in a separate stack and hand this stack to the paraeducator, who will record them.

4. Write Clear Steps for Peers

Below, write out clear steps for what you want peers to do. Use this list of steps as a guide as you prepare directions for peers.

Go through a stack of 10 flash cards two times. The first time, use a 0-second delay. The second time, use a 4-second delay.

0-second delay	4-second delay
1. *Hold up flash card*	1. *Hold up flash card*
2. *Prompt answer and wait for a response*	2. *Wait 4 seconds for a response*
3. *If student is correct, provide praise* *If student is incorrect, prompt answer*	3. *If student is correct, provide praise* *If student is incorrect, prompt answer*

5. Logistics

How many peers will provide tutoring?	When will tutoring occur?
Two	*When peers finish independent work early*
Who will provide training and coaching?	When will peer training occur?
Paraeducator	*During lunch*

Identify a Target. The first step is identifying an academic target for which the student would benefit from short and frequent practice, beyond what is currently provided in the general education classroom. Sometimes, there might be an opportunity to shift practice with teachers or paraeducators in a separate classroom into the regular education classroom. Other times, there may be a new opportunity to target a skill that is rarely practiced.

There are several guidelines to keep in mind when selecting skills. First, the skill should be aligned with the general education curriculum and/or a goal from the student's IEP. Second, it is best to choose skills that can be practiced quickly and that have clear right and wrong answers. Open-ended skills that take longer and involve subjective judgement, such as creative writing, do not lend themselves well to peer tutoring. Instead, focus either on skills with simple discrete responses (e.g., basic math facts, identifying letter sounds, defining a vocabulary word) or a skill that can be mastered by using the same sequence of steps. For example, if a student is learning to "count on" with a number line when adding, steps might include (1) identify the larger number, (2) place finger on the corresponding number on the number line, (3) count out the smaller number and move finger to the right one time for each number, (4) record the sum, which is where your finger ended. Third, select a skill that peers have either already mastered or design a way for them to check answers. For example, if a peer is going to tutor a student on basic math facts, the peer would need either to have already mastered the math facts or to use flash cards that include the correct answer on the back.

Select an Instructional Approach. Select an instructional approach that the peers can use to target the skill. It is best to select an approach that research has proven to be effective and that is simple and straightforward enough that peers can use it successfully. This chapter features two approaches that meet these criteria—time delay and least-to-most prompting (Neitzel & Wolery, 2009a, 2009b).

Time delay involves two phases that are distinguished by how much time passes between an opportunity to respond and prompting the correct answer. At first, there is a 0-second delay. In other words, the peer prompts the correct answer immediately after providing an opportunity to respond. The goal of prompting immediately is to ensure that the student provides the correct answer and does not make any mistakes. For example, a peer might hold up a flash card with "2 + 3" and immediately say "2 + 3 = 5." The student would repeat back "2 + 3 = 5." After the student is successful with a 0-second delay, the peer begins to provide time for an independent response before prompting. For example, a peer might hold up a flash card with "2 + 3" and wait 4 seconds for the student to provide an independent response. If they provide an incorrect response or no response at all, the peer prompts the correct response by saying "2+3=5" and the student would repeat the answer back to the peer. In both phases, the trial finishes with a correct student response and the peer providing praise. See Table 6.1 for additional examples of how peers might use time delay to target academic skills as well as how the process might look different based on whether students are speaking or responding in another way (e.g., selecting a correct response from a field of choices).

Least-to-most prompting involves providing an opportunity to respond independently followed by a series of prompts that provide increasing amounts of support. For example, a peer would first provide an opportunity for a student to spell "cat" independently. If the student were unsuccessful, they would provide the first letter ("c"). If still unsuccessful, the peer would provide the first two letters ("c-a"). If still unsuccessful, the peer would provide all three letters ("c-a-t"). The trial ends when the student provides the correct response and the peer provides praise.

When choosing between time delay and least-to-most prompting, there are two key points to consider. First, least-to-most prompting provides multiple opportunities for mistakes, while time delay is designed to reduce mistakes by immediately prompting the correct answer. Therefore, if high rates of errors are a concern, time delay might be a better choice (Collins, 2012). However, if the student has already partially mastered a skill and an immediate prompt would be unnecessary, least-to-most prompting might make more sense. Second, adopt the approach that is most likely to be implemented correctly (Cook & Odom, 2013). If a paraeducator will be training the peers and that paraeducator is experienced in one approach but not the other, choose the approach that they already know well. Similarly, if peers have already been taught to use one approach, consider planning for them to use the same approach when working on a new skill or with a new student.

Design a Data Collection System. A critical part of peer tutoring is to collect data on the student's progress to inform whether the instructional approach is working or if changes might be needed. There are a variety of approaches for collecting data, and the best choice is often the one that is most accurate with the least amount of extra effort. Older peers might be able to record the accuracy of the student's responses on a data collection sheet during the tutoring session. Younger peers who are using flash cards might be able to sort the cards into stacks of correct and incorrect responses, then hand the two stacks to a teacher or paraeducator who records them on a data sheet. In other cases, the student with a disability might be able to self-record their own data or an adult may need to probe the student and record their responses. If a peer will be responsible for data collection, this should be included in the peer directions that are discussed in the next section.

TABLE 6.1 Examples of Time Delay Steps for Different Skills and Communication Profiles

Step	Example: Sight words for a speaking student	Example: Sight words for an AAC-user
Phase: 0-second delay		
Opportunity: Provide an opportunity for the student to respond	Peer holds up a sight word flash card that says "you"	Peer puts 3 flashcards on table and asks, "Which one says 'you'?"
Prompt: Immediately prompt the correct answer	Peer immediately says "you"	Peer immediately points to the card that says "you"
Wait: Wait for the student to provide the correct answer	Peer waits 4 seconds for a response	Peer waits 4 seconds for a response
Respond: Praise the student for providing the correct answer After an incorrect or no response, reprompt the correct answer	If the student says "you," the peer says, "Yes, it's you" If student does not say "you," the peer says "you" again and waits for a response	If the student points to the card that says "you," the peer says, "Yes, that's you" If student does not point to the card that says "you," the peer points to "you" again and waits for a response
Phase: 4-second delay		
Opportunity: Provide an opportunity for the student to respond	Peer holds up a sight word flash card that says "you"	Peer puts 3 flashcards on table and asks, "Which one says 'you'?"
Wait: Wait for the student to provide the correct answer	Peer waits 4 seconds for a response	Peer waits 4 seconds for a response
Respond: Praise the student for providing the correct answer After an incorrect or no response, reprompt the correct answer	If the student says "you," the peer says, "Yes, it's you" If student does not say "you," the peer says "you" and waits for a response	If the student points to the card that says "you," the peer says, "Yes, that's you" If student does not point to "you," the peer points to "you" and waits for a response

Example: Math facts for a speaking student	Example: Math facts for an AAC-user
Peer holds up a math flash card that says 4 + 3	Peer holds up a flash card that says 4 + 3 and gestures to a number line
Peer immediately says "7"	Peer immediately points to "7" on the number line
Peer waits 4 seconds for a response	Peer waits 4 seconds for a response
If the student says "7," the peer says, "Perfect, 4 + 3 is 7" If the student does not say "7," the peer says "7" again and waits for a response	If the student points to "7," the peer says, "Perfect, 4 + 3 is 7" If the student does not point to "7," the peer points to "7" again and waits for a response
Peer holds up a math flash card that says 4 + 3	Peer holds up a flash card that says 4 + 3 and gestures to a number line
Peer waits 4 seconds for a response	Peer waits 4 seconds for a response
If the student says "7," the peer says, "Perfect, 4 + 3 is 7" If the student does not say "7," the peer says "7" and waits for a response	If the student points to "7," the peer says, "Perfect, 4 + 3 is 7" If the student does not point to "7," the peer points to "7" and waits for a response

Write Clear Steps for Peers. Next, write out steps for peers in a way they will understand. For examples of what peer directions might look like, see Figure 6.2 for directions for time delay to teach math facts and Figure 6.3 for least-to-most prompting for listening comprehension.

FIGURE 6.2 Sample Directions for Peers to Use Time Delay to Teach Math Facts

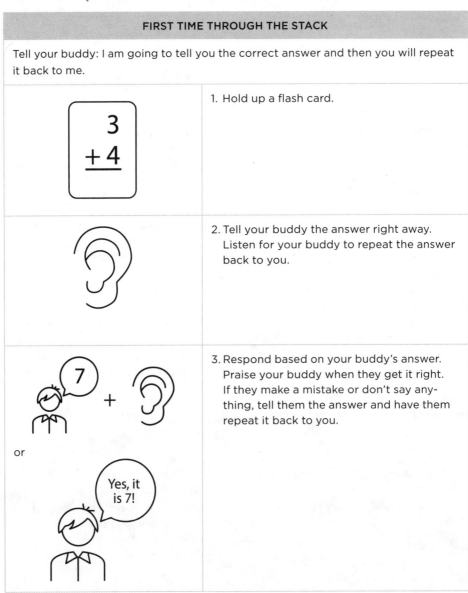

FIRST TIME THROUGH THE STACK	
Tell your buddy: I am going to tell you the correct answer and then you will repeat it back to me.	
3 $+\,4$	1. Hold up a flash card.
	2. Tell your buddy the answer right away. Listen for your buddy to repeat the answer back to you.
7 + or Yes, it is 7!	3. Respond based on your buddy's answer. Praise your buddy when they get it right. If they make a mistake or don't say anything, tell them the answer and have them repeat it back to you.

SECOND TIME THROUGH THE STACK

Tell your buddy: This time you will try it on your own, but I will help if you get stuck.

	1. Hold up a flash card.
	2. Listen for your buddy's answer.
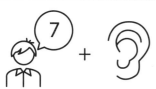 or 	3. Respond based on your buddy's answer. Praise your buddy when they get it right. If they make a mistake or don't say anything, tell them the answer and have them repeat it back to you.

FIGURE 6.3 Sample Directions for Peers to Use Least-To-Most Prompting to Support Listening Comprehension

HOW TO USE LEAST-TO-MOST PROMPTING
After you finish reading the story, tell your buddy: I am going to ask you questions about what we read. If you have trouble, I will give you a little help at first and then more help if you need it.

Who is Meg trying to find? + (ear)	Ask the question. Wait a few seconds for your buddy to answer. If they answer correctly, Skip to Step 5. If not, go to Step 2.
Meg missed her father and would stop at nothing to find him. Even if that meant traveling through time and space. + (ear)	Reread the paragraph that contains the answer. Wait a few seconds for your buddy to answer. If they answer correctly, skip to Step 5. If not, go to Step 3.
Meg missed her father and would stop at nothing to find him. + (ear)	Reread the sentence that contains the answer. Wait a few seconds for your buddy to answer. If they answer correctly, skip to Step 5. If not, go to Step 4.
her father + (ear)	Say the answer and point to it in the text. Wait a few seconds for your buddy to answer. If they answer correctly, go to Step 5. If not, repeat this step.
That's right! Awesome listening!	Praise your buddy for listening and getting the right answer.

Note: This example of least-to-most prompting is adapted from the procedures described in Hudson et al. (2014).

Work as a Team to Sort Out Logistics. As a team, consider logistics for what peer tutoring will look like. Decide whether peer tutoring will always be provided by the same peer or if this role will be shared by multiple students. Think about when peer tutoring will be provided. Sometimes, peer tutoring can be naturally embedded within routines that are already established. For example, a peer who often finishes their independent work early might tutor a student while they are waiting for other students to finish. In other situations, a regular education teacher might see value in providing a designated time when *all* students work in partners, but the peer tutoring during that time would be individualized for the student with a disability. For example, most third-grade students work in pairs on multiplication facts while the student with a significant disability works with a peer on addition facts.

In addition, consider who will provide peers with training and coaching and when initial training might occur. If a regular education teacher or paraeducator will provide training, ensure that they are skilled at the instructional approach before they train peers. Peer training should take only about 20 minutes and could occur over lunch, during downtime in class, or at another time that the regular education teacher agrees to.

Train Peers

See Figure 6.4 for a checklist of how to train peers. Like anyone who is learning to use a new teaching strategy, it is critical to explain, model, and have peers practice each step of the strategy. Peer training should not conclude until the peers have demonstrated, through role play, that they are able to implement the strategy as intended.

FIGURE 6.4 Peer Training Checklist

☐ **Share Goals**

Explain that the purpose of peer tutoring is to give their buddy extra practice with something they are working on. Share the specific skill that they will be working on with the buddy. Explain that, at the same time, peer tutoring gives the peers experience teaching someone else and keeping track of what they have learned. These skills will be valuable as peers get older and take more responsibility for their own learning.

☐ **Share Timing**

Tell peers when tutoring will occur, how long it will take, and how many times it will happen.

☐ **Share and Explain the Written Steps**

Provide the steps that explain how the peers should tutor their buddy. Walk through each step individually, and explain what each step means.

☐ **Model the Steps**

Have another adult or one of the peers pretend that they are the buddy who will receive tutoring. Model all the steps they should use while teaching their buddy.

☐ **Peers Practice Through Role Play**

Pretend that you are the buddy receiving tutoring, and have the peers practice teaching you.

☐ **Provide Feedback**

Highlight what the peers did well and what, if anything, they could do to improve. Anchor your feedback to the written steps. Give peers extra opportunities to role play until they can do all the steps correctly.

☐ **Preview Coaching**

Tell peers that you will be there to help them every time they provide tutoring and that they can always come to you with questions. Explain that sometimes you will provide tips and hints for how they can adjust their tutoring.

Monitor Progress and Make Data-Based Decisions

To ensure that peer tutoring is effective, teachers will need to monitor student progress and make data-based decisions. Regularly review the student's data to gauge if (1) the student is making progress and no changes are needed, (2) the student has mastered content and is ready to move on to something new, or (3) the student is not making progress and adjustments should be made to the peer tutoring strategies (Collins, 2012).

Observe and Provide Coaching

Peers will need ongoing support beyond the initial training, so an adult will need to provide feedback and address their questions and concerns. This adult will need to be present regularly in the regular education classroom and be fluent in the instructional strategy so that they understand what the peers are doing well and what they should do differently. Often this adult is a special education paraeducator. It is especially important for this person to observe peers and provide feedback during the first few times the peer and student work together. This is an opportunity to make sure that the peer gets into a habit of following the directions correctly and that both the peer and the student feel confident and successful.

Troubleshooting

Peer tutoring often goes very smoothly, but sometimes coaching involves working through challenges. The following case studies illustrate examples of challenges and how they can be resolved.

CASE STUDY 1: Maria always waits until I tell her the answer.

PROBLEM. Nathan has been helping Maria practice her subtraction facts for a few weeks. He is using time delay. This means he starts out by immediately prompting her to the correct answer, and then later gives her a chance to respond without help. The problem is Maria *never* responds without being prompted. Nathan talks with Ms. Brown, the paraeducator who trained him how to tutor Maria. He tells Ms. Brown, "Maria always waits until I tell her the answer. I don't think she is learning anything."

SOLUTION. Ms. Brown suggests that they try a small adjustment to the tutoring. She tells Maria, "Maria, this time we are going to do things a little differently. Nathan is going to hold up the flash card and we will see if you know the answer without any help. I really need you to tell us your best guess of what the answer is. If your best guess is not quite right, Nathan will tell you the right answer. But he needs to hear your best guess before he gives you any help."

OUTCOME. Ms. Brown and Nathan are surprised that not only does Maria begin responding independently to every math fact, but she is correct most of the time. Out of the ten math facts that she is working on, there are only two that she does not know. Ms. Brown and Nathan agree that he should continue to encourage Maria to give her best guess and wait on her to provide a response before helping. Given that Maria seems to have already mastered most of the math facts they were working on, Ms. Brown prepares new flash cards to add to the rotation.

CASE STUDY 2: I am not sure what Jason is saying.

PROBLEM. Sam is excited to help Jason learn new sight words, but the first day of tutoring does not go how he expected. He holds up flash cards, but when Jason reads them aloud, Sam is not always sure what Jason is saying. He asks Ms. Robertson for help.

SOLUTION. Ms. Robertson asks Sam to go through all the words with Jason again while she watches. As she watches, Ms. Robertson sees that Sam can understand what Jason is saying most of the time—the problem occurs with words that have specific sounds that are hard for Jason to say. After going through fifteen flash cards, Sam was only unsure of what Jason said three times. Ms. Robertson talks with Sam. She explains that she can understand what Jason is saying and that when he does provide an answer it is usually right. She tells Sam that it took a lot of practice for her to understand Jason and that she is sure that over time he will understand more of what Jason is saying too.

In the meantime, she suggests that Sam just check with Jason to make sure he said the correct word. For example, if Jason provides and unclear answer when looking at the word "you," Sam could ask, "Did you say 'you?'" If Jason says yes, then Sam should praise him for getting it right. Sam looks puzzled. "What if he didn't know the right answer but he just says he did?" Ms. Robertson smiles and says, "I like how you are thinking like a teacher." She explains that there are a couple of reasons why this is not a big concern. First, when she was watching, Jason usually did not say any answers that were incorrect. He did not know all the words, but when he did not know a word, he usually would not say anything. So, it is most likely that when he does respond, his answer is correct. Second, even if Jason does say he said the right answer even though he did not, he is still going to hear the right answer multiple times when Sam asks him if he said it and then says the answer again when he praises him. So, no matter what, Jason is going to be learning.

OUTCOME. Sam tries the new approach that Ms. Robertson suggested, and things go more smoothly. Jason, who has a lot of experience with being misunderstood, clearly appreciates when Sam gives him the benefit of the doubt on words that are tricky to say. Sam feels a lot more confident after having more practice and with having a strategy to use when he is not sure what Jason said. As time goes on, Sam does not need to use this strategy very often because he begins to understand more of what Jason is saying.

CASE STUDY 3: This is getting old.

PROBLEM. For the past few months, Desmond has been helping Kaitlyn practice defining vocabulary words from biology class. One day, Desmond surprises the classroom teacher, Mr. Pearson, by telling him, "I used to like working with Kaitlyn, but it is getting old. Do I have to keep doing it?"

SOLUTION. Mr. Pearson thanks Desmond for coming to him. Mr. Pearson asks Desmond if he wants to quit working with Kaitlyn completely or if he just does not want to work with Kaitlyn every day. Desmond looks surprised. It had not occurred to him that it would be an option to work with Kaitlyn only some days.

Mr. Pearson and Desmond work together to recruit four more peers who might enjoy working with Kaitlyn. Mr. Pearson trains the four peers in the instructional strategy. He has Desmond come to the training, and Desmond is excited to provide pointers about working with Kaitlyn. Mr. Pearson makes a tutoring schedule, and each of the five tutors works with Kaitlyn one day of the week. Desmond's day is Tuesday.

OUTCOME. When Mr. Pearson checks in with Desmond, he says that things are going great. He no longer feels like working with Kaitlyn is a chore—instead, it is something he looks forward to doing each week. Also, after helping Mr. Pearson train the other peers, Desmond sees himself as an important member of a team.

Partnering With Paraeducators

Often, a special education teacher will not be able to be present in a general education classroom to train and coach peers to provide peer tutoring. In these situations, they may need to depend on the regular education teacher and/or paraeducator who is already supporting the student in the classroom. When partnering with paraeducators, there are proven training and supervision strategies that set them up to be successful (Brock & Anderson, 2021). These include defining roles, explaining how the intervention will benefit the student, walking through a checklist of steps, modeling the steps, and observing and providing feedback. This section describes how to apply each of these strategies to peer tutoring.

Define Roles

It is the teacher's responsibility to plan and design the intervention. This means the teacher is responsible for identifying students who would benefit from tutoring, identifying peers who will provide the tutoring, designing the instructional strategy, and designing the data collection system. In their leadership role, it is appropriate for teachers to solicit input from the paraeducators, especially in situations where the paraeducators might be more familiar with peers and the regular education classroom. Appropriate roles for paraeducators include implementing the initial peer training, coaching peers as they tutor, and assisting with data collection. Teachers should be explicit about which of these roles they are asking paraeducators to do.

Talk About the Benefits for the Student

Describe how peer tutoring allows students to get extra academic instruction without leaving the regular education classroom. Also explain that although peer tutoring is designed as an academic intervention, it often promotes interactions between students with significant disabilities and their peers that would not otherwise occur.

Walk Through the Checklist

Provide paraeducators with a completed planning sheet (Figure 6.1) and the checklist for the initial peer training (Figure 6.4). Walk through each component of the planning sheet and checklist while providing explanations and examples of what each step entails.

Model the Steps

Paraeducators are most likely to implement the steps as designed if they have observed a teacher do it first. With the paraeducator observing, implement the initial peer training, and provide coaching to peers on the first day that peer tutoring is implemented. Paraeducators can be active observers by following along with the checklist from Figure 6.4.

Observe and Provide Feedback

Observe the paraeducator while they implement their first initial peer training, when they coach a peer for the first time, and then intermittently over time. Use the implementation checklist as a guide for supporting the paraeducator during the initial peer training. If the paraeducator misses one of the steps, the teacher can step in to help make sure that it gets covered. If the problem was just forgetting a step, the teacher might simply point to the step to remind the paraeducator. If the paraeducator is unsure what to do, the teacher might model implementation of that step.

Helping a paraeducator to provide coaching during tutoring can be more challenging. The paraeducator will need to supervise and gauge the degree to which the peer is implementing the strategy as intended and to provide feedback as needed. Sometimes a teacher may need to encourage a paraeducator to jump in and provide more coaching and modeling, and other times they may need to direct a paraeducator to give the peer and student more space. Also, it sometimes takes practice for paraeducators to give feedback in a way that feels constructive and not critical. It might be helpful to share the troubleshooting examples above to give paraeducators a sense of what their coaching could look like.

Peer Tutoring in Action

The following vignette, a composite of real experiences, illustrates what peer tutoring looks like in action. At the beginning of this chapter you read about Jordan, a third-grade student who received literacy instruction in a regular-education classroom. Jordan's parents hoped that his teachers would find ways for him to receive more of his instruction in the regular education classroom, including instruction focused on phonics and sight words. Below you'll read how Jordan's teacher, Ms. Donovan, used peer tutoring to allow Jordan to practice these skills with his peers in the inclusive classroom.

Ms. Donovan shares that she heard about an approach called peer tutoring but that she has never tried it before. She explains that peer tutoring would help Jordan to get extra practice on things like phonics and sight words by working with his peers and that these peers would be trained and supervised by Mr. Gilmore—the special education paraeducator who goes to the regular education class with Jordan. Peer tutoring could be one way to help Jordan progress with his early reading skills while spending more time in the regular education classroom. Jordan's parents love this idea and are eager to hear how things go.

Ms. Donovan sets up a meeting with Mr. Gilmore and Mrs. Rawlings—the regular education classroom teacher. Ms. Donovan explains that she would like to start using peer tutoring to give Jordan some extra practice on his reading skills and that together they would plan what the peer tutoring will look like, when it will happen, and which peers will be involved. She says she thinks a peer could use a strategy called time delay to practice sight words with Jordan. She shares that time delay is a proven strategy and that it would only take about five minutes for a peer to practice with Jordan. Ms. Rawlings starts to think about natural times in the classroom schedule when peers could work with Jordan. Her mind goes to the class's morning routine, when students have morning work and then can choose between reading a book or working on their creative writing projects while they wait on their classmates to finish. There are several students who consistently finish their work early, so perhaps working with Jordan could be another free choice for them. The team agrees that after peers finish their own work, one peer will practice sight words with Jordan for five minutes. Ms. Rawlings talks individually with three peers who often finish their work early and confirms that they would be interested in working with Jordan as a free choice.

Ms. Donovan meets with Mr. Gilmore to walk him through the checklist for how to train peers. She explains that because he has never seen a peer tutor training before, she will lead this one and he can observe and jump in when he has something to add. That way, he will be ready to run similar peer trainings in the future. She also explains that the strategy that the peers will use—time delay—is the same strategy that Mr. Gilmore is already using to practice many different skills with students in their special education classroom. So he is well positioned to help coach the peer to use this approach. She gives him a copy of the instructions for peers, walks him through it, and asks if he has any questions. She explains that after the initial training he will be supervising the peers and that it will be important for him to compliment them when they do things well, provide feedback if they struggle to follow the directions, and be available to talk with them if they have questions or concerns.

The next day, Ms. Donovan and Mr. Gilmore meet with three peers while the rest of their class is in related arts. Ms. Donovan starts by thanking the peers for volunteering to help. She explains that peer tutoring is going to help Jordan with his reading and that she will give them strategies for teaching and keeping track of progress that may be helpful to them in the future. She explains that working with Jordan will be a free choice for them after the finish their morning work, that it will only take about 5 minutes, and that she is hoping that one person will work with Jordan each day. Next, she hands written instructions to the peers and walks through each step. With Ms. Donovan pretending to be Jordan, Mr. Gilmore models how to do each step. Then, the peers take turns trying out the strategy, with Ms. Donovan continuing to be the student. Mr. Gilmore jumps in to compliment the peers when they do things well. When something is not quite right, he models how to do it correctly and has the peer repeat what he did. After practicing a couple of times, all three peers have the steps down. At the end of the training, Ms. Donovan explains that Mr. Gilmore will be there to help when they *work with Jordan. Mr. Gilmore assures them that they can always come to him with questions and that he sometimes may give them tips and tricks.*

The next morning, the first peer finishes their morning work and asks Mr. Gilmore if she can work with Jordan. Mr. Gilmore gets out the materials she needs and gets them set up. The peer does fantastic but seems a little nervous. Mr. Gilmore smiles and gives her a thumbs up to encourage her. When she is done, she hands Mr. Gilmore a stack of all the sight words that Jordan got correct on his own, and Mr. Gilmore records them on a data sheet. Things go well with the other two peers also. Mr. Gilmore does step in once to remodel 0-second time delay for one peer, and then the peer picks it up right away. Ms. Donovan checks in regularly with Mr. Gilmore to see how things are going and to look at Jordan's data. Jordan is making slow and steady progress. After about two weeks, he has demonstrated mastery of more than half the words, and Ms. Donovan gives Mr. Gilmore a list of new words to make into flash cards.

Ms. Donovan sends a note home to Jordan's parents to let them know how well things are going. She shares how much progress Jordan has made, how much he enjoys working with his peers, and how much they enjoy working with him. Ms. Donovan begins to think about opportunities to use peer tutoring with her other students.

Conclusion

Peer tutoring is a way to provide supplemental academic instruction while keeping students in the regular education classroom and creating opportunities for students to interact with their peers. Peers who provide tutoring can benefit by learning new teaching skills and new ways to track learning—skills that will serve them well when studying for a test or tutoring others. Peer tutoring typically involves a special education teacher, regular education teacher, and a paraeducator working closely together. Together, they can ensure that students get extra practice on important goals while remaining in an inclusive classroom.

FIGURE 6.5 Blank Initial Planning Sheet for Peer Tutoring

Identify an Academic Target

What academic skill will be the focus on peer tutoring? This should be one or more academic skills for which the student would benefit from short and frequent opportunities to practice, beyond what is already provided in the regular education classroom.

Identify an Instructional Approach and Design Steps for Peers

What instructional approach will peers use to target the skill? Consider using proven approaches, such as time delay or least-to-most prompting. Record the name of your approach below.

Design a Data Collection System

Describe how you plan to collect data on student progress. Will peers, teachers, or the student be responsible for recording correct responses?

Write Clear Steps for Peers

Below, write out clear steps for what you want peers to do. Use this list of steps as a guide as you prepare directions for peers.

continues

Logistics

How many peers will provide tutoring?

When will tutoring occur?

Who will provide training and coaching?

When will peer training occur?

7

Scaling Up and Combining Approaches

The previous chapters in this book provide step-by-step guides for implementing peer-mediated interventions for students with significant disabilities. These are powerful tools that can improve social and academic outcomes for students with significant disabilities in inclusive classrooms, lunchrooms, and at recess. Like any tool, each is designed for a specific purpose. Peer support arrangements promote social interaction and academic participation, FLIP recess improves communication and play outcomes at recess, peer networks build social connections outside the classroom, and peer tutoring can promote progress on academic goals.

Given that each is specialized, it is unrealistic to expect one tool to do more than it was designed to do. For example, it is not reasonable to expect peer support arrangements implemented in a biology class to generalize to increased socialization at lunch (Schaefer et al., 2018a). In addition, a tool does not work when it is not being used. For example, when peer support arrangements are used effectively in a social studies class, this usually does not translate into increased interaction or participation in a physical education class—even when the same peers are present in both classes (Brock et al., 2016).

Therefore, the best way to promote meaningful inclusion across the school day is to use a combination of tools that are well-matched to their purpose (Schaefer et al., 2018b). For example, a second-grader might receive peer tutoring on phonics during literacy centers, peer support arrangements during science instruction, FLIP recess, and a peer network intervention at lunch. Similarly, a high school student might benefit from peer support arrangements during multiple class periods and a peer network intervention during a period designated for club meetings. When teachers match tools to inclusive situations across the school day, they can maximize the positive impact of inclusion on students with significant disabilities. See Figure 7.1 and Figure 7.2 at the end of the chapter for sample and blank planning tools for matching peer-mediated interventions to different situations across the school day.

FIGURE 7.1 Sample Completed Matrix for Matching Peer Mediated Interventions With Inclusive Activities or Settings Across the School Day

| INCLUSIVE ACTIVITY OR SETTING | PEER-MEDIATED INTERVENTIONS | | | |
	PEER SUPPORT ARRANGEMENT	PEER NETWORK INTERVENTION	FLIP RECESS	PEER TUTORING
Literacy centers				X
Social studies instruction	X			
Lunch		X		
Recess			X	
Related arts classes	X			

At the same time, it is okay to start small and build up. It is unwise for a novice to start out by simultaneously implementing several different peer-mediated interventions across multiple students. A better approach might be to try one intervention for a single student before extending it to multiple students or adding a new intervention. This kind of scale-up dovetails with effective strategies for training and supervising paraeducators. For example, after a teacher has provided extensive modeling and feedback on peer support arrangements in one classroom, a paraeducator will need less initial support to train and coach peers in other classrooms. In the short term, replicating the same approach across different students and situations will make an immediate impact without requiring teachers to start at square one with learning and training paraeducators to implement a new strategy. Given the demands that are packed into a teacher's day, it is prudent to be strategic and ensure that the process for combining and scaling up peer-mediated interventions is feasible and sustainable.

Scaling Up and Combining Approaches in Action

The following two vignettes—both composites of experiences from real teachers and students—illustrate what it can look like to scale up and combine peer-mediated interventions. The first focuses on an elementary school.

Lincoln Elementary

Ms. Jackson teaches in a resource room for students with significant disabilities at Lincoln Elementary. She is excited about how well peer support arrangements are going for Cory, a second-grade student with multiple disabilities. She is proud of how Ms. Nelson, a paraeducator on her team, has shifted the way that she supports Cory in the regular education classroom. During social studies and science, Ms. Nelson used to sit next to Cory at a table in the back of the classroom. Now Cory sits at a desk, like all the other students, and is flanked by three peers who have volunteered to provide support. Ms. Nelson checks in with the peers at the beginning of activities, helps them figure out how they will support Cory to participate while also completing their own work, and then supervises from a distance as Cory and his peers work together. Cory's communication in the class has dramatically increased, including use of a computer that he uses as an augmentative and alternative communication (AAC) device.

The success of Cory's peer support arrangement during social studies and science has Ms. Jackson excited about the potential of peer-mediated interventions for other students and for Cory at other times of the school day. Part of her wants to try to start everything at once, but she settles on a more realistic plan to slowly scale up her use of peer-mediated interventions. First, she considers that she already has a process down for training paraeducators to facilitate peer support arrangements, and Ms. Nelson already shines in how she facilitates during social studies and science in Cory's class. With this in mind, she decides to first focus on scaling up peer support arrangements for other students and for Cory before turning to other peer-mediated interventions. This involves developing plans and training two other paraeducators who work with different students. In addition, she develops a plan for Ms. Nelson to facilitate peer support during Cory's time in related arts classes (music, physical education, library, and computer lab). She often pops into classrooms to observe and provide feedback, and she also begins to lean more heavily on the regular education teachers to supervise paraeducators as they grow more confident in their understanding of peer support arrangements. It takes several months to get peer support arrangements up and running for all students who would benefit.

Next, Ms. Jackson works to prioritize another peer-mediated intervention that could be used to benefit multiple students. She lands on FLIP recess, given that all her students attend recess with peers without disabilities. She works with an administrator to get staff coverage in her classroom for an hour so that she can provide initial training to all three paraeducators at the same time. She explains to the paraeducators that she will take responsibility for the video modeling in the classroom and is looking to them to coach peers at recess. This is the first time that Ms. Jackson has been able to train more than one paraeducator at the same time, and she is pleasantly surprised by how the training is enhanced by paraeducators learning from each other and brainstorming ideas as a group. After initial training, Ms. Jackson looks forward to visiting the playground to see how things are going. She is impressed by how some of the paraeducators are applying principles they learned from peer support arrangements to coaching peers on the playground.

Sometimes she provides suggestions and models strategies, but more often she finds herself praising her staff and helping them troubleshoot when they come to her with concerns.

There are only a few months left of school, and Ms. Jackson knows that it will be a busy time, with testing and wrapping up the school year. She celebrates the progress that her team has made toward making Lincoln Elementary a more inclusive school where students with significant disabilities and their peers benefit from learning and playing together. She has plans to go further—perhaps by setting up peer network interventions for some students during lunch—but this will have to wait until next year.

By combining interventions, such as peer support arrangements and FLIP recess, teachers can facilitate meaningful inclusion for multiple students across multiple settings. As illustrated in the case study, it is pragmatic to achieve initial success with a single intervention and student before working to expand. Also, once paraeducators achieve success with one peer-mediated intervention, they are often able to transfer some of the skills they learned to new approaches.

Northside Middle School

Peer-mediated interventions look different in middle and high schools compared to elementary schools. Students have distinct class periods when they go to different classrooms; breaks between classes become a new opportunity for social interaction; and there is no recess. With these differences in mind, the following vignette illustrates what it might be like to scale up peer-mediated interventions in a middle school.

Mr. Chamberlain, a special education teacher at Northside Middle School, just finished getting a peer network intervention up and running. Now, one of his students on the autism spectrum, Julia, loves going to lunch on Tuesdays and Thursdays. Those are the days that a paraeducator on Mr. Chamberlain's team facilitates a peer network intervention.

Previously, Julia sat with only the paraeducator and another student with a significant disability at a table on the edge of the cafeteria. Now, Julia sits with five girls who have volunteered to eat lunch with her. They spend the first half of lunch eating and chatting, and then they do something fun together for the last few minutes before the bell rings. Mr. Chamberlain loves when he gets a chance to pop into lunch and see how things are going. Julia and her new friends clearly enjoy each other's company.

Given how successful the peer network intervention was for Julia, Mr. Chamberlain starts to think about opportunities to expand his use of peer-mediated interventions for Julia and his other students. He thinks carefully about how he could do this feasibly and efficiently. He decides to start by gradually putting peer network interventions into place for all his students with significant disabilities. This starts with a lot of planning and training, but it gets easier after all his paraeducators have received their initial training and some coaching. For some students, network meetings happen at lunch, like for Julia, but for other students this happens during a study hall or a club meeting time. Having meetings happen in different contexts, along with staggering meetings for different days of the week, helps Mr. Chamberlain make sure that his staff is not stretched too thin at these times.

It takes several months to get peer network interventions up and running for all his students, and Mr. Chamberlain begins to think about other ways to promote interactions between his students and their peers. He remembers that Julia is really enjoying her biology class, but for her to grasp the concepts, they are spending a lot of time teaching her vocabulary in the special education classroom. He wonders if the biology teacher might be open to working with him to set up peer tutoring for Julia so she could get some extra practice in the class with the vocabulary words she needs to understand. Not only is the biology teacher receptive to this idea, but she wants to take things a step further. She says that all her students would benefit from extra practice learning new vocabulary for each unit. They agree that all students will work with partners to practice defining vocabulary words for the first five minutes of each class and that Julia will have an individualized list of words with simplified definitions. Most students just quiz each other and tell each other if they are right or wrong, while two peers are taught to use a time delay procedure when working with Julia. Mr. Chamberlain is encouraged by how receptive the biology teacher was to peer tutoring, and the two of them work to put peer tutoring in place for another student with a significant disability who takes biology during a different period of the day.

At a staff meeting, Mr. Chamberlain and the biology teacher copresent on how peer tutoring on content vocabulary has helped students, both those with and without disabilities. After the meeting, several other regular education teachers come up to Mr. Chamberlain. They ask if he would be willing to work together to set up peer tutoring in their classes too.

For middle and high school students, peer network interventions are a great place to start when scaling up peer-mediated interventions. Given the increased prominence of peer relationships in adolescence, focusing efforts on building social connections is especially important. In addition, supporting a peer network intervention during lunch tends to be easier than peer support arrangements during an academic class period. Focusing on an easier and simpler intervention can help a team experience more immediate success that they can build on.

Conclusion

These vignettes illustrate how teachers can scale up and combine peer-mediated interventions to maximize their impact across students and the school day. They also show what feasible implementation looks like. Often, a good starting point is one peer-mediated intervention for a single student. After initial success, teachers can think strategically about how to scale up and branch out in ways that are the most feasible and make the biggest impact. Becoming highly skilled at peer-mediated interventions—as with any teaching strategy—takes time and effort. But given the potential of peer-mediated interventions to enhance the quality of inclusion, it is more than worth it. After all, it isn't inclusion without peers.

FIGURE 7.2 Blank Matrix for Matching Peer Mediated Interventions With Inclusive Activities or Settings Across the School Day

	PEER-MEDIATED INTERVENTIONS			
INCLUSIVE ACTIVITY OR SETTING	PEER SUPPORT ARRANGEMENT	PEER NETWORK INTERVENTION	FLIP RECESS	PEER TUTORING

References

Amadi, C., Brock, M. E., Barczak, M. A., & Anderson, E. J. (2022). Improving social and play outcomes for students with significant disabilities during recess. *American Journal on Intellectual and Developmental Disabilities*. Advance online publication. https://doi.org/10.1352/1944-7558-127.5.400

Anderson, E. J., & Brock, M. E. (2020). Being in the right place at the right time: Educational placement of students with intellectual disability by state and year. *Inclusion, 8*(3), 210–221. https://doi.org/10.1352/2326-6988-8.3.210

Asmus, J. M., Carter, E. W., Moss, C. K., Biggs, E. E., Bolt, D. M., Born, T. L., Bottema-Beutel, K., Brock, M. E., Cattey, G. N. Cooney, M., Fesperman, E. S., Hochman, J. M., Huber, H. B., Lequia, J. L., Lyons, G. L., Vincent, L. B., & Weir, K. (2017). Efficacy and social validity of peer network interventions for high school students with severe disabilities. *American Journal on Intellectual and Developmental Disabilities, 122*(2), 118–137. https://doi.org/10.1352/1944-7558-122.2.118

Biggs, E. E., Carter, E. W., Bumble, J. L., Barnes, K., & Mazur, E. L. (2018). Enhancing peer network interventions for students with complex communication needs. *Exceptional Children, 85*(1), 66–85. https://doi.org/10.1177%2F0014402918792899

Biggs, E. E., Gilson, C. B., & Carter, E. W. (2016). Accomplishing more together: Influences to the quality of professional relationships between special educators and paraprofessionals. *Research and Practice for Persons with Severe Disabilities, 41*(4), 256–272. https://doi.org/10.1177/1540796916665604

Brock, M. E. (2018). Trends in the educational placement of students with intellectual disability in the United States over the past 40 years. *American Journal on Intellectual and Developmental Disabilities, 123*(4), 305–314. https://doi.org/10.1352/1944-7558-123.4.305Brock, M. E. (2022). A Guide to Implementing Recess-Based Peer-Mediated Intervention. In E. E. Biggs & E. Carter (Eds.), *The Power of Peers*. TIES Center. https://publications.ici.umn.edu/ties/peer-engagement/practice-guides/recess

Brock, M. E., & Anderson, E. J. (2021). Training paraprofessionals who work with students with intellectual and developmental disabilities: What does the research say?. *Psychology in the Schools, 58*(4), 702–722. https://doi.org/10.1002/pits.22386

Brock, M. E., & Carter, E. W. (2016). Efficacy of teachers training paraprofessionals to implement peer support arrangements. *Exceptional Children, 82*(3), 354–371. https://doi.org/10.1177%2F0014402915585564

Brock, M. E., & Huber, H. B. (2017). Are peer support arrangements an evidence-based practice? A systematic review. *The Journal of Special Education, 51*(3), 150–163. https://doi.org/10.1177/0022466917708184

Brock, M. E., & Schaefer, J. M. (2015). Location matters: Geographic location and educational placement of students with developmental disabilities. *Research and Practice for Persons with Severe Disabilities, 40*(2), 154–164. https://doi.org/10.1177%2F1540796915591988

Brock, M. E., Barczak, M. A., Anderson, E. J., & Bordner-Williams, N. M. (2021). Efficacy of tiered training on paraeducator implementation of systematic instructional practices for students with severe disabilities. *Exceptional Children, 87*(2), 217–235. https://doi.org/10.1177%2F0014402920947641

Brock, M. E., Biggs, E. E., Carter, E. W., Cattey, G. N., & Raley, K. S. (2016). Implementation and generalization of peer support arrangements for students with severe disabilities in inclusive classrooms. *The Journal of Special Education, 49*(4), 221–232. https://doi.org/10.1177%2F0022466915594368

Brock, M. E., Cannella-Malone, H. I., Seaman, R. L., Andzik, N. R., Schaefer, J. M., Page, E. J., Barczak, M. A., & Dueker, S. A. (2017). Findings across practitioner training studies in special education: A comprehensive review and meta-analysis. *Exceptional Children, 84*(1), 7–26.

Brock, M. E., Carter, E. W., & Biggs, E. E. (2019). Supporting peer interactions, relationships, and belonging. In F. Brown, J. McDonnell, & M. Snell (Eds.), *Instruction of Students with Severe Disabilities, Ninth Edition.* Pearson.

Brock, M. E., Dueker, S. A., & Barczak, M. A. (2018). Brief report: Improving social outcomes for students with autism at recess through peer-mediated pivotal response training. *Journal of Autism and Developmental Disorders, 48*(6), 2224–2230. https://doi.org/10.1007/s10803-017-3435-3

Brock, M. E., Shawbitz, K. N., Anderson, E. J., Criss, C. J., Sun, X., & Alasmari, A. (2021). Recess Should Include Everyone: a Scoping review of interventions designed to improve social and play outcomes for elementary students with developmental disabilities at recess. *Review Journal of Autism and Developmental Disorders, 1*–12. https://doi.org/10.1007/s40489-020-00233-8

Carter, E. W., Asmus, J., Moss, C. K., Biggs, E. E., Bolt, D. M., Born, T. L., Brock, M. E., Cattey, G. N., Chen, R., Cooney, M., Fesperman, E., Hochman, J. M., Huber, H. B., Lequia, J. L., Lyons, G., Moyseenko, K. A., Riesch, L., M., Shalev, R. A., Vincent, L. B., & Weir, K. (2016). Randomized evaluation of peer support arrangements to support the inclusion of high school students with severe disabilities. *Exceptional Children, 82*(2), 209–233. https://doi.org/10.1177%2F0014402915598780

Carter, E. W., Moss, C. K., Asmus, J., Fesperman, E., Cooney, M., Brock, M. E., Lyons, G., Huber, H. B., & Vincent, L. B. (2015). Promoting inclusion, social connections, and learning through peer support arrangements. *Teaching Exceptional Children, 48*(1), 9–18. https://doi.org/10.1177%2F0040059915594784

Carter, E. W., Sisco, L. G., Brown, L., Brickham, D., & Al-Khabbaz, Z. A. (2008). Peer interactions and academic engagement of youth with developmental disabilities in inclusive middle and high school classrooms. *American Journal on Mental Retardation, 113*(6), 479–494. https://doi.org/10.1352/2008.113:479-494

Collins, B. C. (2012). *Systematic instruction for students with moderate and severe disabilities.* Paul H. Brookes Publishing Company.

Cook, B. G., & Odom, S. L. (2013). Evidence-based practices and implementation science in special education. *Exceptional Children, 79*(2), 135–144. https://doi.org/10.1177%2F001440291307900201

Coyne, P., Pisha, B., Dalton, B., Zeph, L. A., & Smith, N. C. (2012). Literacy by design: A universal design for learning approach for students with significant intellectual disabilities. *Remedial and Special Education, 33*(3), 162–172. https://doi.org/10.1177/0741932510381651

Dell'Anna, S., Pellegrini, M., Ianes, D., & Vivanet, G. (2020). Learning, social, and psychological outcomes of students with moderate, severe, and complex disabilities in inclusive education: A systematic review. *International Journal of Disability, Development and Education*, 1–17. https://doi.org/10.1080/1034912X.2020.1843143

Frantz, R., Douglas, S., Meadan, H., Sands, M., Bhana, N., & D'Agostino, S. (2022). Exploring the professional development needs of early childhood paraeducators and supervising teachers. *Topics in Early Childhood Special Education, 42*(1), 20–32. https://doi.org/10.1177/0271121420921237

Giangreco, M. F. (2010). One-to-one paraprofessionals for students with disabilities in inclusive classrooms: Is conventional wisdom wrong? *Intellectual and Developmental Disabilities, 48*(1), 1–13. https://doi.org/10.1352/1934-9556-48.1.1

Gilmour, A. F. (2018). Has inclusion gone too far? Weighing its effects on students with disabilities, their peers, and teachers. *Education Next, 18*(4), 8–17.

Herbert, M. E., Brock, M. E., Barczak, M. A., & Anderson, E. J. (2020). Efficacy of peer-network interventions for high school students with severe disabilities and complex communication needs. *Research and Practice for Persons with Severe Disabilities, 45*(2), 98–114. https://doi.org/10.1177%2F1540796920904179

Hochman, J. M., Carter, E. W., Bottema-Beutel, K., Harvey, M. N., & Gustafson, J. R. (2015). Efficacy of peer networks to increase social connections among high school students with and without autism spectrum disorder. *Exceptional Children, 82*(1), 96–116. https://doi.org/10.1177%2F0014402915585482

Hudson, M. E., Browder, D. M., & Jimenez, B. A. (2014). Effects of a peer-delivered system of least prompts intervention and adapted science read-alouds on listening comprehension for participants with moderate intellectual disability. *Education and Training in Autism and Developmental Disabilities, 49*(1), 60–77. http://www.jstor.org/stable/23880655

Hume, K., Steinbrenner, J. R., Odom, S. L., Morin, K. L., Nowell, S. W., Tomaszewski, B., McIntyre, N. S., Yucesoy-Ozkan, S., & Savage, M. N. (2021). Evidence-based practices for children, youth, and young adults with autism: Third generation review. *Journal of Autism and Developmental Disorders, 51*(11), 4013–4032. https://doi.org/10.1007/s10803-020-04844-2

Individuals With Disabilities Education Improvement Act (IDEIA). 20USC §1400 (2004)

Jameson, J. M., McDonnell, J., Polychronis, S., & Riesen, T. (2008). Embedded, constant time delay instruction by peers without disabilities in general education classrooms. *Intellectual and Developmental Disabilities, 46*(5), 346–363. https://doi.org/10.1352/2008.46:346-363

Jimenez, B. A., Browder, D. M., Spooner, F., & Dibiase, W. (2012). Inclusive inquiry science using peer-mediated embedded instruction for students with moderate intellectual disability. *Exceptional Children, 78*(3), 301–317. https://doi.org/10.1177%2F001440291207800303

Kurth, J. A., Lyon, K. J., & Shogren, K. A. (2015). Supporting students with severe disabilities in inclusive schools: A descriptive account from schools implementing inclusive practices. *Research and Practice for Persons with Severe Disabilities, 40*(4), 261–274. https://doi.org/10.1177/1540796915594160

Kurth, J. A., Morningstar, M. E., & Kozleski, E. B. (2014). The persistence of highly restrictive special education placements for students with low-incidence disabilities. *Research and Practice for Persons with Severe Disabilities, 39*(3), 227–239. https://doi.org/10.1177%2F0022466919855052

Ley Davis, L., Spooner, F., & Saunders, A. (2022). Efficacy of peer-delivered mathematical problem-solving instruction to students with extensive support needs. *Exceptional Children*, Advance online publication. https://doi.org/10.1177%2F00144029221098764

Lichte, A., & Scheef, A. R. (2022). Exploration of Training Needs of Paraprofessionals to Support Students with Disabilities. *Journal of Special Education Apprenticeship, 11*(1), 1–15. https://scholarworks.lib.csusb.edu/josea/vol11/iss1/5

Light, J., & McNaughton, D. (2012). Supporting the communication, language, and literacy development of children with complex communication needs: State of the science and future research priorities. *Assistive Technology, 24*(1), 34–44. https://doi.org/10.1080/10400435.2011.648717

Matson, J. L., Dempsey, T., & LoVullo, S. V. (2009). Characteristics of social skills for adults with intellectual disability, autism and PDD-NOS. *Research in Autism Spectrum Disorders, 3*(1), 207–213. https://doi.org/10.1016/j.rasd.2008.05.006

Murray, R., Ramstetter, C., Devore, C., Allison, M., Ancona, R., Barnett, S.,Gunther, R., Holmes, B. 2., Lamont, J., Minier, M., Okamoto, J., Wheeler, L., & Young, T. (2013). The crucial role of recess in school. *Pediatrics, 131*(1), 183–188. https://doi.org/10.1542/peds.2012-2993

Neitzel, J., & Wolery, M. (2009a). *Steps for implementation: Least-to-most prompts.* Chapel Hill, NC: National Professional Development Center on Autism Spectrum Disorders, Frank Porter Graham Child Development Institute, The University of North Carolina.

Neitzel, J., & Wolery, M. (2009b). *Steps for implementation: Time delay.* Chapel Hill, NC: The National Professional Development Center on Autism Spectrum Disorders, Frank Porter Graham Child Development Institute, The University of North Carolina.

Pierce, K., & Schreibman, L. (1995). Increasing complex social behaviors in children with autism: Effects of peer-implemented pivotal response training. *Journal of applied behavior analysis, 28*(3), 285–295. https://doi.org/10.1901/jaba.1995.28-285

Schaefer, J. M., Cannella-Malone, H., & Brock, M. E. (2018a). Effects of peer support arrangements across instructional formats and environments for students with severe disabilities. *Remedial and Special Education, 39*(1), 3–14.

Schaefer, J. M., Cannella-Malone, H., & Brock, M. E. (2018b). Promoting social connections across environments for students with severe disabilities. *Career Development and Transition for Exceptional Individuals, 41*(3), 190–195. https://doi.org/10.1177%2F2165143417737073

Shih, W., Dean, M., Kretzmann, M., Locke, J., Senturk, D., Mandell, D. S., Smith, T., & Kasari, C. (2019). Remaking recess intervention for improving peer interactions at school for children with autism spectrum disorder: multisite randomized trial. *School Psychology Review, 48*(2), 133–144. https://doi.org/10.17105/SPR-2017-0113.V48-2

Trausch, K. J., Brock, M. E., & Anderson, E. J. (2021). Efficacy of paraeducators facilitating peer support arrangements for elementary students with multiple disabilities. *Remedial and Special Education,* Advance online publication. https://doi.org/10.1177/07419325211063607

Travers, H. E., & Carter, E. W. (2022). A systematic review of how peer-mediated interventions impact students without disabilities. *Remedial and Special Education, 43*(1), 40–57. https://doi.org/10.1177%2F0741932521989414

U.S. Department of Education. (2022). IDEA Section 618 data products. https://www2.ed.gov/programs/osepidea/618-data/index.html

Wallace, T., Shin, J., Bartholomay, T., & Stahl, B. J. (2001). Knowledge and skills for teachers supervising the work of paraprofessionals. *Exceptional Children, 67*(4), 520–533. https://doi.org/10.1177%2F001440290106700406

Wiggs, N. B., Reddy, L. A., Bronstein, B., Glover, T. A., Dudek, C. M., & Alperin, A. (2021). A mixed-method study of paraprofessional roles, professional development, and needs for training in elementary schools. *Psychology in the Schools, 58*(11), 2238–2254. https://doi.org/10.1002/pits.22589

Williamson, P., Hoppey, D., McLeskey, J., Bergmann, E., & Moore, H. (2020). Trends in LRE placement rates over the past 25 years. *The Journal of Special Education, 53*(4), 236–244. https://doi.org/10.1177%2F0022466919855052

Index

About the Author

Matthew E. Brock is an associate professor of special education at Ohio State University. His research focuses on promoting inclusion by supporting interactions between students with and without disabilities. Matt currently leads a clinical trial of FLIP Recess, an intervention to support inclusion at recess.

Prior to receiving his doctorate, Matt worked as a preschool teacher, elementary school teacher, and taught through the U.S. Peace Corps. He has published more than 50 peer-reviewed journal articles and has been awarded over $6 million in federal grants. In 2021, Matt was named in Stanford University's list of the Top 2% of Scientists Worldwide.